Hu Jintao: Facing China's Challenges Ahead

HU JINTAO: FACING CHINA'S CHALLENGES AHEAD

Andy Zhang

Writers Club Press
San Jose New York Lincoln Shanghai

Hu Jintao: Facing China's Challenges Ahead

All Rights Reserved © 2002 by Andy Zhang

No part of this book may be reproduced or transmitted in any form or by any means, graphic, electronic, or mechanical, including photocopying, recording, taping, or by any information storage retrieval system, without the permission in writing from the publisher.

Writers Club Press
an imprint of iUniverse, Inc.

For information address:
iUniverse, Inc.
5220 S. 16th St., Suite 200
Lincoln, NE 68512
www.iuniverse.com

ISBN: 0-595-22622-1

Printed in the United States of America

Dedication

With my full heart of gratitude, I want to thank my wife Michelle for her countless hours of editing work and valuable insight.

Contents

Chapter 1 1
Chapter 2 12
Chapter 3 22
Chapter 4 31
Chapter 5 39
Chapter 6 44
Chapter 7 54
Chapter 8 58
Chapter 9 63

INTRODUCTION

Nothing on the market can rival the book—Hu Jintao: Facing China's Challenges Ahead. This sweeping biography reveals this mysterious Chinese leader—from his ambitious youth in Qinghua University to the vanguard of political reform. The book discloses the astonishing truth about China: rampant corruptions in the government, tensions across the Taiwan strait, controversial Tibet issues, the environment crisis, unemployment, poverty, AIDS, and the volatile US-China relations.

1

Who is Hu Jintao? Some European reporters prior to China's Vice President Hu Jintao's arrival in Great Britain asked this question in late 2001. Prior to his departure to Western Europe, he gave no direct interviews to western media. Even for Chinese experts in America, Hu Jintao is a mysterious and cryptic leader. Little is known by the outside world about his policy and personality.

Hu Jintao was born in December 1942 in Jixi, Anhui province. The phenomenally rapid Japanese occupation of most of China's east coast since 1937, and constant civil wars, steeped China in economic depression and political chaos. In China, some people call Hu Jintao's generation, "the generation of the People's Republic." He grew up in the time when the People's Republic of China was established and China was no longer under any foreign power. This generation experienced the excitement of the 1950s, and the difficulties and confusions of the 1960s and 1970s. They also witnessed the rapid social and economic development in the last two decades.

As a teenager, Hu Jintao dreamed of studying at China's best college. Hu Jintao's hometown, Jixi, is a beautiful area surrounded by the spectacular Qingliang Mountains. The highest peak is 5897 feet above sea level. The mountain was named for its fresh air and cool climate, for

Qingliang in Chinese means "cool and refreshing." The area is abundant in peaches and other products. It is also a residential area for many generations of brilliant intellectuals and reclusive poets.

Entering China's most prestigious Qinghua University was certainly his turning point in life. He was interested in water conservation and studied hydraulic engineering at Qinghua. He adapted to the university lifestyle very quickly. Many female schoolmates found him effortlessly attractive. He has a photographic memory. He performed well academically and got along with people very well. He was one of the members of the university dance team. In addition, he likes to play Ping Pong—a popular sport in China. Hu Jintao also enjoyed reading classical and contemporary novels. His active reading allowed him to write and speak eloquently. Hu Jintao was successful inside and outside of the classroom. He also met his wife Liu Yongqing at Qinghua University.

His personal goals changed significantly during his college years. Prior to his admission into the Qinghua University, he intended to be an engineer, but he gradually shifted his attention to politics. Qinghua University has a solid tradition of providing political leaders to the government. He joined Communist Party of China (CPC) in 1964. Based on his excellent academic performance and his great interpersonal skills, he was one of the few students hired by the university as a researcher and political instructor right after he graduated in 1965. As always, it was an honor to be hired by China's prestigious university.

Unfortunately, the academic environment declined sharply due to Cultural Revolution. Two years after this Cultural Revolution, in 1968, a decade of political upheaval began. The government sent him off to the poor and remote Northwest province of Gansu to be "re-educated." He performed manual labor with the housing construction team of Liu Jia Xia Engineering Bureau under the Water and Utility Department. He was also shocked by the poverty in the area. Nevertheless, he found great emotional support from his wife Liu Yongqing. She was his closest friend and firm supporter.

Later in 1968, after almost a year as a manual laborer in Gansu province, Hu Jintao joined an engineering bureau of the Ministry of Water Resources and Electric Power, as a technician. Sometimes, life takes an upward swing from the lowest point. From his technician position, he was promoted to office secretary and deputy Party secretary. The position of office secretary and deputy secretary allowed him to gain deeper understanding of government work and party affairs. His hard work ethic and intelligence were well recognized by his supervisor and co-workers. In 1974 he was promoted to secretary of the Gansu Provincial Construction Commission and became deputy head of the Project Design Management Division. In 1980, he became the deputy director of the Gansu Provincial Construction Commission. A person's career development often becomes stagnant at this level, but Hu Jintao continued to rise.

In 1982, at the age of 39, Hu became an alternate member to the 12th China Communist Party Central Committee, the youngest of that body. That year, he was also elected to the Secretariat of the Gansu Provincial Committee of the Chinese Communist Youth League (CCYL). The Youth League is often perceived as the reformist segment of the government and provides potential advancement opportunities for senior level positions.

Hu Jintao soon transferred to Beijing. After arriving in Beijing, Hu joined the Secretariat of the Central Committee of the CCYL and became president of the All-China Youth Federation. In November 1984, he was promoted to the head of the CCYL Secretariat, the top post of China's largest youth organization. Hu Jintao's experience with

China's youth work also enabled him to have a better understanding of the country's younger generation. He once noted that in the process of China's reform, Chinese youth should not only have a sense of urgency and a sense of mission, but also a good understanding of the hardships and complicated nature of the reform. "Do not cherish excessively high expectations while your psychological capacity to bear upon is low," he was quoted as saying.

He had to leave Beijing again at age 42. In 1985, he became the Secretary of the CPC Guizhou Provincial Committee. He was the youngest senior provincial official at that time. He started economic reform in the poverty-stricken Guizhou Province. Within two years, he had visited 86 counties, cities and prefectures in this poor southwestern province. He once said economic development in poverty-stricken areas requires people's dedication. His effort for broad ranged reform gained notable popularity. His name appeared on the authoritative national newspapers such as *People's Daily* and *Guangming Daily*. In addition, he also became political commissar of the Guizhou military region. As early as 1987 he became a full member of the 13th CPC Central Committee—China's top decision-making body.

In 1988, Hu Jintao became the Secretary of the CPC in Tibet. Hu Jintao became Tibet's first non-military party leader. As soon as he arrived in Tibet, he gave the region much more liberal policies than ever. Tibetans were allowed to hang and fly the Tibetan independence flags and take part in other minor political displays. Unfortunately, the pro-independence movements in Tibet's capital city, Lhasa, quickly became very violent. During a bloody riot in March 1989, more than 40 people were killed and several police injured. Hu Jintao had to move more troops into the region to keep the area under peaceful order.

Despite the harsh natural conditions on the Tibet Plateau, Hu Jintao visited many areas and made extensive contacts with people in various circles. Hu Jintao emphasized the region's ethnic unity, social stability and economic growth. Finally, Hu Jintao developed "altitude sickness"—headache, dizziness, fatigue, shortness of breath, loss of appetite, nausea, and disturbed sleep. He returned to Beijing to recuperate after working 18 months on the 12,000-foot plateau.

Once in Beijing, Hu Jintao started working on many critical tasks with key party organization boards and interacted with senior party leaders. The 14th Communist Party Congress in the spring of 1992 was a landmark for both Hu Jintao and President Jiang Zemin. When Hu Jintao entered the Standing Committee of the Political Bureau of the 14th Central Committee of the Communist Party of China (CPC), he was the youngest member in this top decision-making body of the CPC. During the Party Congress, Hu Jintao was elected as Standing Committee member of the Political Bureau of the CPC Central Committee member of the Central Committee's Secretariat. Jiang Zemin was officially elected as General Secretary of CPC—the top post in the Chinese government.

Since then, Hu Jintao has risen quickly into one of the most powerful leaders in the Chinese government. In 1993, he became the President of the Party School of the CPC Central Committee which supervises, educates, and trains local and provincial officials. In 1998, he was elected State Vice President giving him both legislative and executive power. In 1999, he was elected vice chairman of the PRC Central Military Commission to govern and participate in the military affairs of China.

Hu Jintao has great communication skills. His former colleagues have said Hu is a very persuasive person, and very good at coping with complicated situations with firm principles and flexible tactics.

Speaking of the basic qualities of a leader, Hu once said, " a good leader must have firm beliefs and lofty pursuits, do solid work, seek no fame or gain, do away with a bureaucratic air and share the feelings of the masses." "A good leader should encourage democracy and also be capable of taking resolute action at critical moments, and must love life," he added.

Hu Jintao is on the reformist side in the Chinese government. As early as 2001, he had already started political reform in Shenzhen—the city adjacent to Hong Kong. Shenzhen is the vanguard of China's economic reform, having seen phenomenal economic growth since the 1980s. The political reform in Shenzhen decentralized the executive functions of the local government. If this preliminary reform has been successful, a wide range of political reform is forthcoming. He also urged provincial governments to promote young cadres into leadership positions.

Hu Jintao appreciates western democratic style problem solving skills. During his speech at the Central Party School, he emphasized the importance of further advancement in China's market economy and integration into the global economy. Hu Jintao is an open-minded leader and encourages government official to learn from other countries. In January 2002, the Chinese cabinet's Development Research Center signed an agreement with Harvard University's John F. Kennedy School of Government to teach mayors and other officials urban planning and economic development skills.

The top foreign policy Hu Jintao endorses is world peace. The Chinese people want peace. During his meetings with leaders in many countries, peace has been the major theme of his speeches. Hu Jintao has spoken with many foreign leaders including ones from Russia, the United Kingdom, France, Spain, Germany, the United States, Vietnam,

Guinea, Syria, Uganda, and Jordan. He repeatedly emphasized the importance of building strategic partnerships with different countries and enhancing economic ties.

Hu Jintao also encourages young people to learn from other countries. Speaking before visiting US President George W. Bush's speech at Qinghua University in February 2002, Hu said that young people are the hope of the country, the future of the world and the fresh force pushing forward Sino-US friendship. "I hope young people in the two countries will increase exchanges, enhance friendship, learn from each other, and work together to promote peace, progress and development of the world," Hu said.

Hu Jintao said China and the United States are both great countries, and the two peoples are both great peoples. The development of the international situation has repeatedly demonstrated that China and the United States shoulder important responsibilities and have extensive common interests in safeguarding peace and stability in the Asia-Pacific region and the world as a whole. Both countries work together to promote regional and global economic growth and prosperity, fight against terrorism and other cross-border crimes, and address environmental deterioration and other global problems. The US-China friendship conforms to the wishes of the people of the two countries and the trend of the times. "As long as the two sides respect each other, treat each other as equals, seek common ground while reserving differences, US-China relations will be able to develop in a healthy and smooth way," he said.

Bridging the country's technology gap and promoting the country's high tech economy has been Hu Jintao's primary interest during his tours in Shanghai and in his conversations with delegates from Zhejiang Province. During his tours of Shanghai's hi-tech district on

November 17, 2000, he visited Shanghai General Motors, Hua-Hong NEC Electronics, and firms in software development and bioengineering. Hu Jintao said science and technology have been the crucial factor for economic development.

Hu Jintao also emphasized community development. He praised the community development in Shanghai's Chengqiao Second residential area in Changning district, Wuli Bridge Community Cultural Center in Luwan district, and Sangcheng Garden area in 2000. He said significant changes have occurred since the last time he visited in 1997. He told local community leaders to sponsor a wide variety of volunteer, cultural, and entertainment programs. He also wanted the community leaders to play an active role in law enforcement and other community services.

Other domestic issues Hu Jintao has focused on includes:

- Speeding up the legislation process. China has to modify more than a thousand law, regulations, and rules just to fulfill its commitments as a WTO member. Many trade barriers will no long exist, some tariffs will be significantly lower, some terminologies will be revised in line with these used in WTO rules. In addition, China has a severe shortage of qualified lawyers and judges that have sufficient legal knowledge of international laws and WTO litigations. Education and training will be crucial for the implementation of the rapidly changing legal environment.

- Fighting crime. Hu Jintao has praised the results of the nation wide Strike Hard campaign to target major criminals. He also wants local governments to put more effort on preventative law enforcement education.

- Increasing the farmers' incomes. With the challenge of quality agriculture products from other countries, Hu Jintao said it is important to help farmers increase their annual income. Otherwise, their production incentives will be discouraged. He also asked the local governments to introduce more science and technology into the production process.

- Continuously working on pressing unemployment issues and delivering workers' social security pensions on time.

- Encouraging the Chinese citizens and non-citizens living overseas to participate in China's policy making and economic development.

Hu Jintao is regarded as the core of the fourth generation of the Communist Party leadership. The fourth generation leaders will push China into further economic and political reform and continue China's current foreign policies. There are significant differences between the fourth generation leadership and the previous generations. Here are some obvious characteristics of the fourth generation leadership:

1. The fourth generation leadership is knowledge based. The first generation leadership lead by Mao Zedong had a strong bias toward promoting the generals and leaders from the Chinese civil war in the 1940s. Scientific and systematic methods will be applied in problem solving. From the Central Party School to local court systems, the fourth generation leadership will be knowledge based. Unqualified personnel will be let go. Seniority in the party is no longer a strong asset for leadership positions or promotions.

2. The fourth generation leadership will be integrated into the international community. They will open further the domestic markets and eliminate trade barriers. With the entry of WTO at the end of 2001,

China has agreed to open more domestic markets to the international community. Many trade barriers will be knocked down and local protectionism will no longer be feasible. The trade barriers will be knocked down in many industries such as banking, distribution, transportation, manufacturing, and insurance. More state enterprises will lose their competitiveness and more employees will be laid off in the short run. China will also cut agriculture product tariffs significantly—forcing the nation's 800-million farmers to face global competition.

3. The fourth generation leadership will focus on technology growth. The fourth generation of leadership will push the country's technology development forward to increase the technology yield in the nation's economy. Scientists, engineers, and professionals will be encouraged to earn higher salaries. For many scholars, especially overseas scholars, more opportunities are opening up. There will be more flexible policies and favorable regulation for them to invest and research. Key personnel will be selected in a democratic fashion from a much broader range with little or no local citizenship restrictions. Copyright laws will be further enforced to protect intellectual rights and innovations.

4. The fourth generation leadership will be under multiple sources of influences for policy making. The fourth generation of leadership cannot make domestic or foreign policies without the influence from various parties. Foreign investors, legislators from Hong Kong and Macao, business leaders and many other interest groups will influence the government's policy making. The first generation leadership was under almost none of these influences. The second and third generation of leadership was under some of these influences but not as much as the fourth generation of leadership. The fourth generation of leadership is also under closer international observance due to its increased interaction and obligation with the international community.

5. The fourth generation leadership is young. Among the four generations, the fourth generation leadership comprises the youngest team. From central government to local government, the fourth generation leadership will promote younger officials into leadership positions.

6. Economic development, domestic stability and peace will be the top priorities for the fourth generation leadership. The fourth generation leadership will be under pressure to continue the double-digit economic growth under a more complex economic environment. A stable domestic environment is crucial to attract investors. Therefore, the fourth generation leadership will work hard on the unemployment issue, to promote social security, and to decrease the crime rate. The fourth generation leadership will also promote world peace and increase its cooperation with other countries.

2

Since 2001, Hu Jintao has put a lot of effort into political reform. One of the key components is to decentralize the executive branch into multiple functions, with multiple people in charge of each function. The purpose of this strategy is not to follow a western style of government, but to improve its efficiency and to prevent corruption. This experiment started in the southern vanguard of market economy, Shenzhen, a city adjacent to Hong Kong. Shenzhen has turned itself from a small fishing village with several thousands residents into a modern metropolis with more than three million residents since the economic reform started in 1980s. The political reform started as early as January 2002 in Shenzhen government. The results of this reform will serves as the trial-and-error foundation for the future political reform Hu Jintao will take.

Rampant corruption in the Chinese government is the biggest threat to the political stability of the ruling Communist Party.

For almost three years, construction workers in Shenyang suburb were working on a special project that they knew little about. Asphalt roads were paved from the main highway to connect the "Grand Palace"—a luxurious mansion that most ordinary people would find difficult to imagine: a giant swimming pool equipped with imported accessories, Swedish sauna bath, an expensive piano, marble floors, a world-class tennis court, upscale furniture, etc.The outsiders did not know who was the owner nor what was inside until the owners were arrested.

On October 10, 2001, two of the highest-ranking officials in Shenyang, provincial capital of Northeast China's Liaoning Province were handed death sentences after being convicted of corruption.Former mayor Mu Suixin was sentenced to death that the court reprieved for two years.The former deputy mayor—Ma Xiangdong was sentenced to be executed. Ma was arrested in July 2000 and accused of squandering 40 million yuan (US$4.8 million) in public money on a gambling spree in Macao, China.The former Portuguese colony returned back to China in 1999.The gambling industry is the main attraction and tax income for Macao.Like Hong Kong, Macao will maintain its local economic autonomy for 50 years after it returning to China.

In China, family relationships and friendships have always played an important role in a person's promotion and benefits.

On November 16, the court in Nanjing, the capital of East China's Jiangsu Province, started to try Ma's wife, Zhang Yafei.The indictment from the local public prosecutors states Zhang, taking advantage of her position as the president of the No 2 Hospital affiliated to the Shenyang Medical College and her husband's position as deputy-mayor of the city, "illegally accepted money and properties from others, and helped others in securing jobs, promotions and in bidding for projects"— *China Daily* reported.Zhang was said to have illegally obtained some 455,000 yuan (US$54,950) between February 1996 and October 2001. Zhang and her husband allegedly procured another 78,000 yuan (US$9,400), US$500 and a mink coat valued at 15,000 yuan (US$1,800) between February 1994 and May 1999.

Six other senior officials were also expelled from the Communist Party of China (CPC) and removed from public positions. The most interesting part of the case was that the scale of involvement was not limited to the executive branch but also to the judiciary branch:

—Jia Yongxiang, former president of the Shenyang Intermediate Court, was convicted of taking massive bribes and kickbacks to support a corrupt life, and wiping out big personal bills with public money.

—Liu Shi, former procurator-general of the Shenyang People's Procuratorate, was accused of taking huge bribes and interfering with the investigation of Ma Xiangdong.

—Jiao Meigui, former vice-president of the Shenyang Intermediate Court, took bribes from local gangsters and speculated with large amounts of public money.

The primary investigation team, Liaoning Provincial Commission for Discipline Inspection (LPCDI) and the Provincial Supervision Department, said these officials were implicated in the corruption case of Mu Suixin.

On December 7, 2001, Beijing police uncovered what is likely to prove China's largest tax fraud case ever involving losses of more than 20 billion yuan (US$2.4 billion) to the state treasury. The *China Police Daily* said the chief suspect set up 28 front companies over the last two years, used them get false tax receipts from a corrupt Beijing official, then sold the receipts to other firms to be offset against genuine taxes. The crime ring obtained more than 20 billion yuan worth of tax receipts between October 1999 and February 2001 and an official at the Beijing State Tax Bureau took millions of yuan in bribes to supply them, it said. More than 100 other suspects in the case were arrested throughout China.

While China is making spectacular progress toward a market economy, many of its officials feel it is almost impossible to resist the temptation of money.The current political system does little to prevent corruption.For senior local and provincial officials, supervision at the same level is nearly non-exist.The supervision from subordinates is ineffective; who wants to upset their boss?Unless you are unlucky, the supervision from the central government is on a case-by-case basis.That is why each year, the corruption cases get more astonishing, the money involved gets larger, and the people associated with those cases are higher level government officials.

Liu Liying, senior commissioner of the Chinese Ministry of Supervision, noted that as China focuses on cracking down on corrupt cases and deterring the trend of corruption, it should also make institutional innovations to reform the old systems, mechanisms and rules in order to prevent corruption from happening and to get rid of it at its very root.

Another aspect of corruption is that many officials are paid too little.Their western counterparts get paid much more than they do for the same positions that they hold.Even if they have many perks such as housing, a private driver, a nice car, and close to no cost healthcare, the amount of salary received is obviously insufficient to do other nice things.Therefore, the trade between power and money become prevalent.Everyone knows that if you want things done quickly and effectively, you need to pay your share.Ordinary people grasp the business fairly quick and the networking of giving and receiving bribes is almost part of the government norm.The receivers can be anybody related to a powerful man or woman, wife, husband, parent, child, grandparent, aunt, uncle, you name it.

The discipline inspection commission of Ningbo municipal government came up with an innovative method to reduce corruption in 2001. It opened a special account in a local bank for officials to turn over so-called "gift money." The officials do not need to give their names or declare the source of the money. On receiving the money, the bank issues a receipt as proof of the official's refusal to keep the bribe. The bank has so far received 918,000 yuan (US$110,600) from over 80 people. A local newspaper praised the system as "the green exit for bribes." But People's Daily argued, "There are regulations and laws on bribery. Refusing bribes is what any cadre should and must do in the first place. Why should the department put the regulations aside and devise such an outlet for bribes?"

The most dangerous business is collaborative corruption among peers, as shown in the Shenyang's mass corruption case that involved many senior officials.Senior officials meet each other at many work and social occasions weekly.If the judiciary officials are corrupted along with executive branch officials, then the combined destruction and danger is much greater than when within a single branch.It is also the hardest type of corruption on which to crack down.With their combined power, they can run the local government anyway they want with no supervision or questions from any other party.In addition, complaints from the third party will be swiftly punished from both sides, leaving the ordinary people with no channel through which to file complaints.Previously, this type of case only happened in small towns, several tiers further away from the central government's control.But Shenyang is the capital of Liaoning province with more than 8 million residents.Apparently, the system's loopholes have caused the level of corruption to go deeper over the years.

To battle corruption, several measures have been suggested and some of them are now in place.Hu Jintao is leading a government think tank to perform research on how to prevent corruption. There are many suggestions that will lead to significant political reform in the country. For example, at the top of the suggestion list was an open election for the local leadership positions. Currently, in most government organizations, promotion is based on a good relationship with your supervisors and coworkers. Family members, relatives, and friends have better chance than others. Fair competition must be introduced to elect capable personnel into the government. This suggestion has been tried in part of Jiangsu Province for local official elections.

Another suggestion on the list is free media. Media can play an important role in discovering and reporting corruption cases so that the corrupted leaders have to face public scrutiny. Although the government still has much control over the media, this situation is changing. With more competition in the media industry, many newspapers are facing the pressure from readers to deliver higher quality, realistic, and objective reports. As a result, scandals are more frequently reported than ever and liberal newspapers have gained popularity over the conservative newspapers.

The first suggestion actually implemented nation wide was to give government officials a raise. At the end of 2001, almost all government employees received a significant raise. Some of them got several raises throughout the year of 2001.

The most important part is political system reform. If the decentralized Shenzhen government works well, Hu Jintao will likely push the reform forward. There have been tremendous worries in the party regarding the reform; stability is one of the top concerns. Stability has always been China's strong suit for attracting foreign investments. Many party members prefer slow and gradual political reform to maintain the country's stability. Any turmoil—despite how good the initial intention was, will scare many investors away.

Putting senior cadres under the gaze of auditors were also on the top of the political reform list. Ministry-level officials are to be audited each year by the National Audit Office to better curb corruption, in effect since 2000.

The economic duty audit focuses on three aspects. One is whether officials have properly fulfilled their economic duties, second is whether they have caused losses by violating financial regulations, and third is whether they have broken any laws. China began to implement economic duty auditing in 1998 in an effort to curb rampant corruption and losses of large amount of State assets due to negligence. Corruption thrives under a lack of efficient supervision.

Since April 2000, the National Audit Office has audited the leaders of six major financial institutions including the four State-owned banks: Bank of China, Industrial and Commercial Bank of China, China Construction Bank, and Agricultural Bank of China.

According to *China Daily*, the National Audit Office expects to launch auditing on all government and Party leaders above county rank around 2002. Economic duty auditing has been very fruitful in the past. A total of 42,000 party and government leaders, and 15,000 enterprise leaders have been audited since 1998. Among them, 200 were deprived of post, 470 were admonished or punished, and 1,010 were transferred to legal departments. On the other hand, more than 3,300 officials have been promoted thanks to their audit results.

Individual behavior concerning a total of 590 million yuan (US$71 million) has been ferreted out and enterprise violations concerning a total of US$96.17 billion yuan (US$11.59 billion) have been exposed.

In addition, Hu Jintao has consistently promoted bringing more young cadres into the government.In a country deeply rooted in Confucius thought, this is rather a challenge.It is especially true for those older leaders who are unwilling to give up their post.Under the Confucius influence, Chinese people pay the deepest respect to the oldest people since they have more experience and wisdom.Unfortunately, with China's rapidly changing business landscape and entering the WTO at the end of 2001, much of their conventional wisdom and experience is outdated.China now desperately needs the talents of those who have the most cutting edge knowledge in many different fields, from international accounting to copyright laws, from anti-dumping to stock market regulations.Many senior officials have little knowledge about the ever-changing rules and regulations, not to mention that they lack full understanding of the potential impact of them.In addition, many senior local officials resist and are reluctant to follow the new rules and make changes.They would rather keep everything the way it is now.Therefore, replacing some of them is a necessity for China.Without highly educated and qualified officials, it is impossible for China's government to keep up with its economic development.

Every summer, the top Chinese leaders conduct meetings in Beidaihe to discuss the most important issues and to make strategic decisions.Right after the senior leaders summit in Beidaihe in the summer of 2001, Hu Jintao called for bold and innovative measures to promote young cadres ahead of the 16th Communist Party congress the following year.Hu Jintao urged cadres to make personnel changes ahead of the congress, which will elect the new leadership. The call by Hu Jintao sent a shock wave throughout the country's local and provincial governments, since personnel changes have always been the most sensitive and critical issues for local and provincial governments.

Knowing their unavoidable fate of retiring, some officials simply accept it, but many others fight back. Their number one strategy is "age balancing." The term "age balancing" comes from the statistics field. If the central government requires the local government personnel to have an average age of less than 50 years old, for example, a local government can simply bring more younger people on board to lower the average age to an acceptable level without retiring anybody. The result is more people get hired but no senior officials get retired.

The national conference for Organization Department is considered the primary decision making meeting for appointing key party personnel. Therefore, any decision made via this conference will carry deep impact nation wide. During the conference, Hu Jintao said, "party committees at all levels must realize the importance and urgency of promoting young cadres." Hu Jintao's presence at the conference indicated that he was in charge of the group overseeing the reshuffling of cadres in the run-up to leadership changes, which will take place at the congress, scheduled to open in autumn 2002. The Organization Department is currently run by President Jiang Zemin's top aide, Zeng Qinghong.

To speed up China's development, local and provincial officers must be knowledgeable. Development in many areas has been slowed down due to local leaders' ignorance. Hu Jintao has worked on leadership training for years at the Central Party School. He emphasized the importance of further advancing China's market economy and integration into the global economy during his speech at the Central Party School. In January 2002, the Chinese cabinet's Development Research Center signed an agreement with Harvard University's John F. Kennedy School of Government to teach mayors and other officials urban planning and economic development skills. Founded in 1936 as the Harvard Graduate School of Public Administration, the School was renamed the John F. Kennedy School of Government in 1966. It has since expanded to become an international center for scholarship and teaching in effective public problem solving and leadership.

China's development depends on the development in all areas. Each area's development largely depends on its leaders. Hu Jintao's challenge is to ensure that local officials are ready to meet the unprecedented challenges and move the economy forward.

3

In China's big cities, seeing a clear blue sky and breathing clean air has become a thing of the past. During the last two decades of industrial and urban development, China has had some of the most serious air pollution in history. According to the World Health Organization report, China has seven out of the ten worst cities for pollution in the world. Sulfur dioxide and soot from coal create acid rain, which falls on 30 percent of the country. An average city in the United States may have 100 micrograms per cubic meter of particulate pollutants per day, but similar size cities in China may have as much as 1,000 micrograms per cubic meter of particulate pollutants per day. This is ten times as many particulate pollutants! The burning of fossil fuels for residential and industrial purposes emits most of these pollutants.

Many residents in China's major cities are burning coal for cooking and heating. The pollutants emitted by coal burning leads to hazardous levels of indoor air pollution. The high outdoor air pollution levels are mainly caused by industrial emissions and automobile exhaust. Lung disease is the leading cause of death in China. Scientific research has proved the correlation between air pollution and lung disease. In the industrial city of Shenyang, up to 17 percent of the deaths above the national average may be linked to pollution, said Devra Davis, senior scientist at the World Resources Institute. David Wheeler of the World Bank's Development Research Group estimated that 940,000 lives are projected to be lost to pollution related illnesses in Chongqing by 2020[1]. If air pollution in many Chinese cities does not improve in the next several years, many people will die.

Water pollution is another major environmental problem in China. Fast industrial development without corresponding wastewater treatment has turned many rivers, canals, and streams into heavily polluted water. Songhua river, once abundant with long white carps, now has killed 95 percent of its fish resources due to high pollution levels. The remaining fish are so poisonous that the health officials have recommended that residents not eat them. According to official data at the end of 2001, about 85% of metropolitan residents and less than 45% percent of rural residents have access to clean and safe water for eating and drinking. Untreated industrial waste also severely pollutes the underground water in many areas.

The contaminated ground water caused 43 million cases of fluorine poisoning in China in the 1990s. This is a nationwide problem. Fluorine poisoning disease, fluorosis, shows up as mottled enamel on teeth with low doses of fluoride. When the doses get higher, the cells may be affected and the tooth structure severely altered. Besides contaminated ground water, fluorine rich tea and the burning of fluorine containing coal are two other major reasons for fluorosis in China.

Besides air and water pollution, other major environmental challenges Hu Jintao will face include:

- An ever-expanding desert. The desert areas in the northwestern part of China are expanding rapidly and devouring millions of acres of farmland. The annual "sand storm" sweeps thousand of miles from Mongolia to the northeastern coast of China. The strength of the sand storm has increased significantly in recent years. During the

2001 sand storm, scientists at the western coast of Canada were able to feel and detect the magnitude of the powerful sand storm. During the 2002 sand storm, some students in South Korea had to stay home due to the incredible low visibility on the streets.China must work with Mongolia and other countries to keep this situation from becoming a global environmental disaster.

- Water shortages affect many parts of the country.For the areas suffering water shortage, agriculture production is unpredictable from year to year.In some extreme cases, all crops dry out soon after being seeded.
- Although the Chinese government has set up a national reservation for parks, and many laws and regulations are in effect, wildlife crimes are still a major threat to endangered species such as tigers.In 1999, the anti-smuggling bureau in Kunming, Yunnan Province has uncovered large-scale illegal shippment of animal parts. Officials of the bureau found more than 2,000 wildlife skins, including 11 tiger skins and more than 100 pieces of leopard skin.There were many pieces of bear, wild yak, and panda skins. They also found heads of wild yaks and monkeys and elephant tusks. Most shocking of all was the discovery, in two packed refrigerators, of frozen bears' paws.

The Chinese legal system is not well suited to protecting wildlife. In China, wildlife protection is under the jurisdiction of many different departments, such as the National Forest Bureau, the Public Security Bureau, the Customs Bureau, the Commerce Bureau, the Department of Medicine and the Department of Airlines. It is hard to tell whose responsibility wildlife protection is and who should act at what time.In addition, much of China's wildlife protection legislation is flawed and difficult to put into effect. Loopholes in the system often allow criminals to escape without substantial punishment.

- The ever increasing need of seafood consumption and fishery development has lead to over fishing in both the East and South China Seas.Two thirds of the major fish species and several of the region's most important fishing areas are fully or over-exploited.Many nursery areas and breeding grounds are being degraded2.This results in the permanent loss of globally significant marine biodiversity and the livelihood of millions of people.
- The booming paper industry, commercial and residential construction, furniture production, and other industries have further depleted the already diminishing forest resources China has.
- Local governments have failed to preserve the historical buildings and structures.Valuable sites have been demolished to allow commercial buildings to be built.Once those traditional buildings are lost, they are gone forever.Experts have labeled these cities as "disaster zones."
- China has one of the lowest recycling rates for materials such as paper, plastic, glass, metal, etc.Many Chinese products have no recycle indicators as do many products in other countries.Establishing a better and more efficient recycling system will allow China to reuse materials and protect the environment.

Hu Jintao is a strong supporter for environment protection.Since the 1990's, the Chinese government has made some successful efforts.China has set up the largest and the most effective environmental improvement system among developing countries.Many natural gas pipelines have been built and some are under construction.Residents are encouraged to burn natural gas instead of coal and cleaner stoves are being used.China now has 7,000 hydropower plants and operates six million square meters of fixed solar panels. Solar heated greenhouses and stoves are becoming more common.[2]

Environment Protection Industry (EPI) was born around the same time as the electronic, computer, petrochemical and household electrical appliance industries. But the "morning sun industry", as EPI is called, is miles behind these industries, which have since become the pillars of the national economy.

China is undergoing rapid economic development, hence neither market capacity nor technology shortage could be the major reasons for EPI's sorry condition.

China has a broad market for EPI. For instance, wastewater drainage, estimated to be about 3.7 billion tons a day, has caused serious pollution problems. The only possible way to solve the problem is to build wastewater treatment plants. Official statistics show that about 10,000 such plants are needed to treat even half of the wastewater. Over 400 billion yuan (US$48.2 billion) is needed for their construction.

China is not strong in EPI's technology development and needs some key technology from abroad. Some of the country's technology can be compared to advanced ones across the globe, such as one to remove dust and to treat industrial pollution. China is capable too of designing urban wastewater treatment projects and manufacturing key equipment independently.

The Lack of funds seems to be the biggest problem facing China's EPI. At present, foreign aid and loans are the source of most funds for urban wastewater treatment projects. Some foreign companies have entered China to sell their technology and products. The dependence on foreign investment and imported technology has seriously hindered the healthy development of China's EPI, or so it seems. Of the 10,000 EPI firms in China, none can be compared to large multinational EPI corporations in terms of scale and business volume.

The real reason for EPI's unhealthy development is the failure of the country to build a mechanism that would suit the market economy and could stimulate the industry's development. China still does not have favorable policies nor the market climate for its EPI to attract advanced technology, big global and domestic capital, and talented personnel.

The market, usually a decisive guiding factor for an industry, is not playing an important role in the Chinese EPI's development, say experts.

Nowadays, most wastewater treatment projects are built by governments and managed by their administrative organizations. Since local governments usually don't have adequate funds, they fail to maintain the projects' normal operations even if they are completed. Ultimately, the projects become burdens on the government. Governments at various levels, as the major investors in such projects, rarely give a good thought to costs and efficiency.

Experts calculate the standard investment for treating a ton of wastewater to be between 600 yuan (US$72) and 1,000 yuan (US$120). But in China it comes to about 1,500 yuan (US$181) to 2,000 yuan (US$240).

So how does one get out of this unhealthy cycle and give the EPI an ideal climate for rapid development? This precisely is the most important topic for some experts and entrepreneurs today.

Experts say the tradition of relying on State finance for the EPI to develop should be replaced by a new and creative mechanism, capable of bringing all the positive factors into play and expanding the industry with funds raised from the market.

Wen Yibo, an environmental engineering industry expert, has proposed that the build-operate-transfer (BOT) method, popular in advanced countries, should be introduced into the construction and management of EPI projects in China. This means that the government wouldn't be the major investor in projects. The right for construction and management will be granted to the enterprises that will recover the investment through the collection of fees.

"The BOT method could be used to speed up the construction and reduce costs," said Wen. According to scientific calculations, projects constructed and managed under the BOT method are expected to cut down 40 percent of the total investment and the operation cost.

The BOT method will help the industry raise funds, too, through various channels from the public. "This will in a way solve the shortage-of-funds problem, the biggest problem the EPI has been facing," Wen said.

"If the BOT method is used widely, China will become capable of treating 50 per cent of its wastewater in 10 years," he said.

Zhang Shiguo, a Beijing Huatai Securities expert, said small- and medium-sized firms, that comprise most of China's EPI, should try to raise funds from the stock market. To attract funds from investors, firms need the following: advanced technology, standard management skills and a high ability for resource allocation and market promotion.

To create a fine climate for EPI's development is an urgent task of the Chinese government, he said. For instance, a reasonable system to speed up and standardize the construction and management of the EPI must be devised. The present management method, under which various departments want to take a share of a project, has caused a lot of problems.

When a project starts, all local governments want it to benefit the local economy. Local construction companies in most cases are the project builders even if they don't have the ability or technical know-how to do so. Such protectionism should be stopped immediately, experts said.

In 2001, China's EPI output value reached 108 billion yuan (US$13 billion) last year, 25 times more than 10 years ago. According to State Economics and Trade Commission statistics, about 10,000 firms are part of the EPI, that is, four times that of 10 years ago. They employ 1.8 million people.

In China, the EPI started taking shape in the early 1970s. It continued on a very small scale for the next several years. Statistics show there were only 2,500 firms in the industry that had an output of 4 billion yuan (US$482 million) in 1992.

China's EPI has enjoyed a fast growth and will be a focus for investments in the next five years. About 700 billion yuan (US$84.34 billion) will be spent, according to *China Daily*, to improve China's natural and environment conditions in the next five years. This will undoubtedly boost the EPI's growth. If the industry continues to grow at an average of 15 per cent a year during the Tenth Five-Year (2001–05) period, its total output value will reach 200 billion yuan (US$24.1 billion) by 2005.

About 55 billion yuan (US$6.6 billion) will come from the production of environmental protection equipment, 95 billion yuan (US$11.45 billion) from the comprehensive usage of resources, and 50 billion yuan (US$6 billion) from EPI's ancillary sector. According to the Tenth Five-Year Plan (2001–05), ecological improvement and environment protection will play an important role in the domestic consumer market.

The sector is still not a key industry in China, but it has great development potential, and is an industry that has seen rapid development worldwide. The industry is showing increased vitality and has become a key economic factor in the United States, Germany, Japan and Canada. In China, EPI's development has not been satisfactory. The government does not have an overall plan to guide the progress of the industry, leading to blind development.

For instance, the State said power plant desulphurization program was very important for technology renovation during the Seventh Five-Year Plan (1986–90). Demonstration projects were set up during the Eighth Five-Year Plan (1991–95) period and an overall implementation plan was made during the Ninth Five-Year Plan (1996–2000). The program has not progressed as smoothly as expected because of lack of specific policies.

Experts want the government's role to be changed in the market economy. Efforts should be made to guide the industry towards a better, brighter future. To better protect the environment, more favorable policies, funding, training and education are required from the Chinese government.

---

1. Whitney Clavin, Prosperous China Faces Environmental Poverty. Washington, DC, February 24, 2000.
2. ENS report, Asian Nations Put Quarrels Aside to Save South China Sea. Bankok, Thailand, March 28, 2001.

4

As early as 7 AM in the city of Shenyang, a group of unemployed workers gathers together looking for jobs. Each of them has a paper board hanging on his chest displaying the skills he has such as "electrical" or "plumbing." The temperature was around 40 degrees Fahrenheit with a strong Northeast wind. Despite the cold weather and the strong wind, they hope to find some employment soon. Across China, high unemployment rates and bitter unemployed workers strike in cities with a high concentration of state enterprises like Shenyang. In the year of 2001 alone, strikes cost millions of dollars in lost money from items like suspended railway traffic. Several homemade bombs were exploded around the country and dozens of peoples were killed as the result.

China's entry into the World Trade Organization (WTO) at the end of 2001 has brought tremendous pressure on the country's human resources market. The statistics from the Ministry of Labor and Social Security indicate that the number of jobless in the country continues to be a vexing problem, with a registered urban unemployment rate of 3.6 per cent at the beginning of 2002. The total number of registered unemployed in urban areas reached 6.81 million by the end of 2001. There are an additional 5.15 million laid-off workers from State-owned enterprises. Rural surplus laborers are estimated to account for 20 percent of the total 800 million rural population. Wang Dongyan, a senior official with the Ministry of Labor and Social Security, said the unemployment "pressure will be around for years."

After entry into the WTO, many Chinese companies are facing keen competition. Efficiency has proved to be one of the biggest factors many Chinese companies fall far behind in compared with their western counterparts. For example, the Bank of China employs six times more employees than the average western banks using the revenue per employee index. In order to be competitive in the world market and attract investors, they have to lay off employees. Many companies are merging with their peers to achieve synergy. Several major airlines have consolidated into three airline groups. This trend will further raise the unemployment rate. In addition, many existing employees will lose their jobs due to their insufficient education and/or skills. Industries like banking, insurance, telecommunications, automobile manufacturing and petrochemicals will certainly require higher educational backgrounds and skill levels.

In the meantime, China's overall labor demand is low. The total number of employment opportunities decreased by 118,000 during the fourth quarter of 2001. Only the service sector saw a 2 per cent increase in job openings, from September to December in 2001. The labor demand in the agricultural and industrial sectors dropped 0.5 and 1.2 per cent respectively during the same period. Although more job opportunities will emerge in the service sector and parts of the manufacturing industry in the coming years, China's overall employment situation will not be optimistic. Laid-off workers from State-owned enterprises, urban unemployed and rural surplus laborers, will continue to make up the bulk of the country's job seekers in the coming years.

Cases of violation of labor laws are increasing in many areas. Dongguan Elegant Top Shoes Co., Ltd is a contractor with Reebok,

Clarks, and Fila. According to Li Qiang's report on China Labor Watch, among the total number of 5,500 to 6,000 employees, only 10 percent are male workers. The factory recruits female workers aged 18–25 and does not recruit male workers. Most of them come from the provinces of Sichuan, Hunan, and Jiangxi, which are considered poor areas. Most of these female workers have education levels of junior high or just primary school. Usually, the workers that are older than 25 can not carry the intensive working burden of the factory. The factory does not recruit male workers even though they would be better suited to the job. This is because male workers are more active. In the nearby factories, it is the male workers that organize strikes and demonstrations.

Chinese labor laws sets the standard of 40 hours per week as usual work hours (see appendix VI), but the factory administration forces the employees to work more than 60 hours per week. The typical daily work hours are as follows:

7:20–11:30 Morning work hours
9:20–9:30 Break
11:30–12:50 Lunch break
12:50–17:00 Afternoon work hours, 10-minute break in between.
17:00–18:00 Dinner break
18:00–21:00 Extended work hours

Referring to the Factory regulations Section 4.4, under usual conditions, employees stay in the factory for 13.2 hours/day including 11 working hours. The employees do not work over time Wednesday and Saturday evenings. The employees work six days a week in the factory equaling more than 60 hours. According to Chinese Labor Law the normal working hours are 40 hours/week with 4 hours of overtime allowed. Extended work hours not exceeding 36 hours per month are allowed only if the extension is called for due to extraordinary circumstances. In reality, the employees have to work overtime for 80 hours per month, 12 months a year.

According to Chinese Labor Law's Article 70, the State shall develop social insurance undertakings, establish a social insurance system, and set up social insurance funds so that laborers may receive assistance and compensations under such circumstances as old age, illness, work-related injury, unemployment and child-bearing. And Article 72 states that the sources of social insurance funds shall be determined according to the categories of insurance, and the practice of unified accumulation of insurance funds shall be introduced. The employer and individual laborers shall participate in social insurance in accordance with law and pay social insurance costs.

A patient with a disease that cannot be cured in the factory medical office can seek medical services outside the factory, but with a limited medical expense budget. The factory does not establish any medical, employment insurance and pension plans. The employees do not have anything after they leave the factory.

According to Reebok's human rights regulations, employees' wages should cover basic living expenses. The fact is that if a worker uses a portion of his or her wage to buy social insurance, he or she cannot cover these basic living expenses. Thus, according to China's labor laws, the factory does not pay the workers' basic living expenses.

The telephone number of the Worker's Union in Dongguan is listed on the factory's bulletin board, but most employees do not know what the Union is. The complaint conduits are referenced in the factory Regulations Section 10.1 and 10.2. There are three complaint conduits in the factory. The employees can complain to the unit supervisor, write a letter to the company through the company's mailbox, or to the clients via the human rights mailbox. This is regulated in Section 10.2 in the factory regulations.

However, more often employees choose not to complain. Because of the work intensity, sometimes the employees cannot meet the quality or quantity requirement. Under these situations, the supervisors will abuse them. If the employees complain about this, the coordinator will come to the manager and the supervisor to verify the employees' complaint. If the situation is deemed true, the factory administration will penalize the supervisor, but the complaining employees are given a tough time by the penalized supervisor. They will be forced to leave the factory. Thus, it is not advisable for employees to complain.

In China, the All China Federation Trade Union (ACFTU) is the only recognized and legitimate trade union and its subordinate branches are deemed as a mass organization of the working class. The ACFTU was first set up in 1925 in Canton and was not legitimized and consolidated until the Chinese Communist Party (CCP) came to power in 1949. The role of ACFTU was defined after Soviet model as a "transmission belt" for the ruling party according to the top-down principle of "democratic centralism". The ACFTU was regarded as a "pillar of the Party", which in practice denoted the subordinate position of the union to the Party. On the one hand, the ACFTU's responsibility was to transmit the Party's ideological line and policies to the working class and to secure their support and compliance. On the other hand, the ACFTU's goals were to unite all workers and protect their interests and promote the welfare of workers. The dual tasks of the union preclude accomplishing the latter goal effectively without bringing conflict with the former one.[4]

The ACFTU engages in the promotion of workers' interests, such as the negotiation of collective contracts with employers to supplement individual contracts. At the national level there is tripartite consultation of top federation officials with counterparts in government and management. However, the ACFTU has not subsequently improved labor rights and labor conditions. The explanation lies in the inherent affiliation with the state. Since the union is established and supported by the government, the goal is always in conformity with that of the state. Hence, there has not been an intense confrontation between the union and management, since, in theory, the ultimate interests of both have been determined by the state.

According to China's Trade Union Law, the Chinese employees in overseas-funded enterprises are entitled to establish trade union organizations[2]. The requirement to set up trade unions in all overseas-funded enterprises in the coastal provinces has been set high on ACFTU's agenda. In May 1994, the ACFTU announced a new campaign to establish unions in all those enterprises, in economic development zones and coastal cities, and to strengthen the power of workers for collective bargaining and rights protection[1]. However, the scope of unionization in the foreign-funded enterprises has remained narrow. By the end of 1995, just over two million employees in such enterprises were unionized[3]. The reasons are as follows. First, most foreign investors are reluctant to establish trade unions in their enterprises because of the fear that unionization will challenge their managerial authority. Second, the ambassadorial role of unions in foreign enterprises serves the Party, and is cooperative. This poses difficulty for the union in asserting bargaining power for the employees[2].

There is another reason worth mentioning as well. Though the Trade Union Law stipulated the necessity for unions to set up a consultative and negotiating system with the administration, participate in democratic management, and represent and defend the rights and interests of employees according to law, there is no supervising organism in place for implementation. In the cases of labor rights and labor law violations previously cited, none of the factories had a workers' trade union in place and none of the workers demanded the establishment of unions to protect their interests. This has put workers in a most vulnerable situation where they are almost always deprived of any bargaining power and subject to the conflicting interests of employers and unions. People regard unions as part of the government or the state mechanism. They never see the union as an important means to bargain for their rights and guard their interests. This is even happening in state owned enterprises whose population accounts for the primary representation of the union.

Though the lack of autonomy in ACFTU is a major issue contributing to the malpractice and labor abuse by foreign corporations, it is not the only factor. Lack of legal institutions regulating China's labor-management relations has created a very favorable environment for foreign investors to conduct business without the countervailing power of organized labor. The large supply of inexpensive labor also inhibits union economic power. Some foreign investors do take advantage of the loopholes in the Chinese legal system during China's economic transitional period when rules governing employment and labor relations are not yet fully in place. When we examine Nike's, Reebok's and Disney's offshore factories in light of international labor standards for multinational enterprises, none of them are living up to the international standards with regards to the use of forced labor, wages, benefits, conditions of work, safety and health, and collective bargaining[4].

The employment issue will be one of Hu Jintao's pressing domestic agenda items to ensure social and financial stability in China. So far, the Chinese government has employed various ways to create jobs for the unemployed, including offering free re-employment services and promoting community services such as housekeeping and milk delivery. The governments at all levels will urge the country's foreign enterprises to hire more employees by offering them preferential policies. The government also encourages private businesses to hire more people. In addition, the government is working on the timely delivery of the pensions of retirees and subsidies for the unemployed. In 2001, the Chinese government delivered a total of 205.4 billion yuan (US$24.7 billion) in pensions, and financial assistance of 34.2 billion (US$4.1 billion). More than 104 million people around the country had benefited from unemployment insurance by the end of 2001—according to the official data.

---

1. Chan, Anita & Senser, Robert. A. 1997. "China's troubled workers." Foreign Affairs, March-April 1997 v76 n2 pp. 104, 118.
2. Hong, Ng S. & Warner, Malcolm. 1998. China's Trade Unions and Management. St. Martin's Press INC. N.Y.
3. White, Gordon. 1996. Chinese Trade Unions in the Transition from Socialism: Towards Corporatism or Civil Society? British Journal of Industrial Relations, September 1996 pp. 433-457.
4. Wang, Yajing. 1999. Employment, Labor Relations, and the Union Situation in China. http://www.mtsu.edu/~ceconed/journal99.htm.

5

In China, there are three million children who drop out of school each year because of poverty. Despite the fast economic development in the past two decades, fighting poverty is still the top agenda for Chinese leaders. In many rural areas, people are very dependent on their yearly harvest from the farmland. Any natural disaster, such as flood or drought, will immediately push them into a food shortage and poverty. Many local governments lack the minimum investment funding to help poor families.

Since the beginning of market reform in 1978, initialized by Deng Xiaoping, many rural areas in China have developed quickly. Some farmers have greatly benefited from the market reform and break up of ownership of farmland into individual's hands. They engage in animal husbandry, agriculture, aquaculture, and orchard production, in addition to raising traditional crops. Newspapers and televisions were eagerly reporting the progress made in the rural areas. A household that has an annual income that exceeds ten thousand yuan was regarded as a role model. At the same time, income disparity appeared within the same region. There are farmers who make more money than their neighbors.

Shortly after the rural area market reform, the market reform in the cities brought the income disparity to the cities as well. With the uncertain future of market economy and the resistance from some hardliners inside the communist party, China opened its first group of twenty-four coastal cities for foreign investment and market economy in the mid 1980s. Favorable investment policies attracted much needed foreign investment into those areas. These areas experienced phenomenal economic growth and the standards of living have risen considerably. Gaining valuable insight and confidence from those developments, China gradually opened all other areas to international investors. Today, the income disparity between coastal cities and inland cities is astonishing. While an average household in Dalian is making over US $2,000 annually, an average household in some inland cities makes only around US $500. Since equality has always been the goal of the Chinese government, the income disparities are very disturbing.

The income disparities between cities and rural areas have created many social problems in China. Because cities have better education, health care, transportation, and other services, millions of farmers have quit farming and moved into the cities. Some people label them as a "floating population." They do not have equal opportunities as city residents. These workers have to work the jobs many city residents are unwilling to take such as construction work, trash recycling, baggage delivery, food service and other types of manual work. Despite their contributions to the cities, they also often suffer lower pay and various restrictions. Most high paying jobs in the cities require local citizenship. There are also discriminations reported in association with some rural workers.

Another alarming trend is selling of farmland for commercial use. Some farmers are allured by the large sum of compensation and sell their farmland for commercial use. In China, farmland areas are diminishing at an alarming rate. To prevent further loss of farmland, the Chinese government has emphasized the need to protect the farmland for the national food supply stability.

There are also significant differences between the east and west regions of China. The east region has more higher education opportunities and more research institutions. As a result, there are more skilled workers and a better technology base. Financially, the east is much better off. Traditionally, the east also has the strongest industrial base and majority of the nation's fixed assets. There is remarkable income disparity between the east and west regions of China.

Since 2000, the Chinese government has initialized "develop the west" projects to close the gap between the east and west. Premier Zhu Rongji has invited many business investors from Hong Kong to tour some western provinces and encourage them to invest in those provinces. The government also plans to build more railways and roads to those provinces in order to improve their infrastructure for future economic development. All these measures would take at least several years to reap the best benefits. In the meantime, many western provinces are continuously losing their most talented people to the eastern provinces.

Hu Jintao worked in several western provinces such as Gansu and Guizhou. Those provinces are underdeveloped. He will continue the effort to bridge the gap between the east and west regions and eliminate poverty.

Arriving in Harbin right before the Chinese New Year in February 12, 2002, Hu Jintao's trip was described by journalists as a "visit to the coldest city in the coldest season."

Strategically located in the northeastern part of Manchuria—Harbin is a city known for its spectacular snow and ice festivals in the winter. Huge ice blocks are cut and moved from the Songhua River to the nearby parks. Artists from all over the world turn them into beautiful ice sculptures. Miles of artistic figures, buildings, towers, and even huge palaces are made of ice with colored lights inside of them. Some of the structures are big enough to allow visitors to go inside of them. It is a world of snow and ice. It is a winter wonderland. Needless to say, Harbin is one of the coldest cities in China.

The three provinces that composed Manchuria—Heilongjiang, Jilin, and Liaoning provinces are well known for their various industries. Most people are employed by state owned factories. With the restructuring of state enterprises and massive lay offs in the recent years, those provinces have millions of unemployed workers. Along with the governor of Heilongjiang Province, Song Fatang, Hu Jintao visited some poverty-stricken families in the region.

Although the total number of people living in poverty has decreased about 90 percent in the past two decades, poverty is still a major source of rural unrest in China. Much rural unrest is tied to the heavy taxation by the local government or the lack of assistance from the local government during the needy years.

The United Nations (UN) World Food Program (WFP) will provide 178,000 tons of food to China from 2002 to 2005. The US$23 million program is designed to cover 2.6 million poverty-stricken people, mainly in the country's remote and mountainous areas in central and western provinces.

The project aims to enable people to increase food production and rural infrastructure through food-for-work activities, including irrigation, land improvement and drinking water supply. Food-for-training programs will be given primarily to women to improve their agricultural skills, literacy and health. According to the agreement, the Chinese Government will cover the transportation and delivery costs for the donated food.

Another UN agency, the International Fund for Agricultural Development (IFAD), will co-finance the project with preferential loans of US$84 million, most of them being small loans to the poor or for use in infrastructure construction. This operational contract is the first one under the WFP Country Program for China 2001–05 that was approved in 2001.

Under the Country Program, WFP promised to provide China's western area with 340,000 tons of wheat in support of integrated rural development and 200,000 tons of food to feed children at school. WFP has been a close partner of the Chinese Government in its efforts to reduce poverty.

Poverty is not only a challenge to the national stability, it is also a threat to the future development of those poor areas. One of Hu Jintao's domestic agenda is to help millions of people escape poverty and hunger.

6

Tibet, located 12,000 feet above sea level, is praised as the Roof of the World. The special geographic conditions and environment cultivated its unique culture, history and people, creating a splendid chapter in the history of human civilization. There are the grand Himalayan Mountains, clear and beautiful mountain high rivers, dreamlike crystal clear lakes on the plateau, and the vast endless grassland in north Tibet. The mysterious Buddhist culture and the warm and open-hearted Tibetans, make Tibet the holy land that stands closest to the blue sky, to cherish the snow-capped mountains, grassland, lakes, glaciers, sunshine, and lamaseries and spiritual home.

Hu Jintao gazed out the streets, buildings, and temples when his private charter was descending over the Lhasa airport. The time was July 19, 2001. It has been fifty years since Tibet became part of the People's Republic of China. The Tibet issue has always been a delicate issue Chinese leaders have to deal with internationally. The Tibet in Exile led by Dalai Lama, is the primary counterpart that the Chinese government has to work with.

Although there are only 131,000 people that belong to Tibet in Exile, it has gained noticeable influence in several countries include the United States. Most of its members live in India—about 100,000 of them. Followed by Nepal—25,000 of them. There are about 1,500 people who live in the United States that belong to Tibet in Exile. Dalai Lama is the spiritual leader of Tibet in Exile. Since 1967, Dalai Lama initiated a series of journeys, which have taken him to more than 40 nations and was awarded The Norwegian Nobel Peace Prize in 1989. In Washington, D.C., at the Congressional Human Rights Caucus in 1987, he proposed a Five-Point Peace Plan as a first step toward resolving the future status of Tibet (see appendix IV).

- **The Historical Issues**

Both the Chinese government and Tibet in Exile agreed that prior to Tibet becoming a part of People's Republic of China, the condition in Tibet were far from desirable. During the meeting with Premier Zhou Enlai in 1954, Dalai Lama indicated, "Tibetans were fully aware of our need to develop politically, socially and economically."

The Chinese government described "the feudal serfdom under theocracy, which had lasted for several hundred years in Tibet, stifled the development of the social productive forces of Tibet, seriously hindered social progress, and relegated Tibet to the state of extreme poverty, backwardness, isolation and decline, to the point of verging on total collapse."

In November, 2001, the Information Office of the State Council issued a white paper in Beijing entitled "Tibet's March Toward Modernization", which reviewed the modernization drive in Tibet over the past 50 years. The 16,000-word white paper is composed of three parts: the Rapid Social Development in Tibet, Tibet's Modernization Achievements, the Historical Inevitability of Tibet's Modernization (see appendix III). The white paper says that even in the mid-20th century, Tibet was still extremely isolated and backward, almost without a trace of modern industry, commerce, science, technology, education, culture and health care. Primitive farming methods were still in practice. The grain yield was only four to 10 times the seeds sown. The rigid hierarchy and savage political oppression, the fetters of religion brought by theocracy, and the imperialists' invasion had led to enormous deaths from hunger and cold, poverty and diseases among the serfs, which made over 95 percent of the whole population in Tibet 50 years ago. Crisis lurked on every side in Tibet."

Regarding the historical position of Tibet, the Dalai Lama emphasized that "it is an established fact that Tibet and China existed as separate countries in the past. However, as a result of misrepresentations of Tibet's unique relations with the Mongol and the Manchu Emperors, disputes arose between Tibet and the Kuomintang and the present Chinese government. The fact that the Chinese government found it necessary to conclude a '17-Point Agreement' with the Tibetan government in 1951 clearly shows the Chinese government's acknowledgement of Tibet's unique position." The Tibet in Exile also indicated, "at times Tibet extended its influence over neighboring countries and peoples and, in other periods, came itself under the influence of powerful foreign rulers - the Mongol Khans, the Gorkhas of Nepal, the Manchu Emperors and the British in India."

There are periods that the Chinese people and Tibetans have suffered great culture destruction such as Cultural Revolution. Those years, for both the Chinese people and Tibetans, were disastrous. However, the unprecedented and unimaginable loss—especially human lives, are unrecoverable. It is just a part of history. The Chinese government never denied its mistake, but the mistake has not been repeated. After all, it was an unfortunate tragedy of human history.

During the 36th Anniversary of Tibetan National Uprising Day, on 10 March 1995 in Dharamsala, Dalai Lama said: "It is my belief that it is more important to look forward to the future than dwell in the past. Theoretically speaking it is not impossible that the six million Tibetans could benefit from joining the one billion Chinese of their own free will, if a relationship based on equality, mutual benefit and mutual respect could be established."

• **The Contemporary Issues**

The Chinese government has listed the following key growth areas in Tibet since 1951:

—The economy in Tibet has progressed significantly over the past 50 years. Tibet is fast on its way toward a modern market economy after having thoroughly abandoned the former closed, natural economy. The region's GDP reached 11.746 billion Yuan (US$1.42 billion) in 2000, twice as much as in 1995 and over 30 times as much as in 1950.

—Modern industry, having grown from nothing, has gradually become an important pillar of the fast economic development in Tibet. The modern industrial system with Tibetan characteristics has cultivated some nationally famous brand names.

—In 2000, the region's total grain output reached 962,200 tons, and the total amount of livestock numbered 22.66 million head. Self-sufficiency in grains and edible oils had been basically realized. The distribution of meat and milk per capita had surpassed that of the national average.

—By 2000, Tibet has set up 25 scientific research institutes, engaging in studies on history, economics, linguistics and religion, as well as Tibetan medicine and pharmacology.

—The number of medical and health organizations in the region has reached 1,237. The cooperative medical service has covered 80 percent of the Tibetan rural areas. The average life expectancy of Tibetan people has risen from 35.5 years in the 1950s to the present 67 years. Tibet's population had increased to 2.5983 million by 2000, or an increase of more than 160 percent over the figure for the early 1950s.

—The white paper says the State invested a huge amount of fund, gold and silver in protecting and maintaining the key historical heritage in Tibet.

—Great progress has been made in standardization of information technology in the Tibetan language. The Tibetan code is the first ethnic minority written language in China to have reached the international standards.

—Radio, TV, telephone and the Internet have become the main methods for the Tibetan people to learn or communicate with the rest of the country and the world.

Differences still exists between the Tibet in Exile and the Chinese government over several issues. Some contemporary issues raised by Tibet in Exile are:

—Human rights. Political persecution includes Tibetans who work for the preservation of Tibetan culture, which includes teaching the Tibetan language and opening private schools. Tibetan cadres and members of the Chinese Communist Party are made to undergo political reeducation, reminiscent of the days of the Cultural Revolution. Those suspected of harboring religious and national feelings are being purged. Monasteries have been raided by the People's Armed Police and the chain of political arrests has now been extended to rural areas. The rebuilding and construction of new monasteries has been prohibited and the admission of new monks and nuns stopped. Tibetan travel agents and tourist guides have been dismissed in order to control the flow of information and Tibetan children are no longer permitted to study abroad. Those who are presently studying abroad have been ordered to return.

—Environment. The economic development in Tibet has caused the decline of its ecological environment in Tibet. Sadly, in the past decades the wildlife and the forests of Tibet have been almost totally destroyed by the Chinese. The effects on Tibet's delicate environment have been devastating. What little is left in Tibet must be protected and efforts must be made to restore the environment to its balanced state.

—Population shift. In the Amdo province, for example, where Dalai Lama was born, there are 2.5 million Chinese and only 750,000 Tibetans. Today, in the whole of Tibet 7.5 million Chinese settlers have already been sent, outnumbering the Tibetan population of 6 million. In central and western Tibet, Chinese sources admit the 1.9 million Tibetans already constitute a minority of the region's population. These numbers do not take the estimated 300,000 - 500,000 troops in Tibet into account - 250,000 of them in Tibet. For the Tibetans to survive as a people, it is imperative that the population transfer is stopped and Chinese settlers return to China.

The respective descriptions from the Chinese government are:

—The Tibetan people's freedom of religious belief and their traditional customs and habits have been respected and protected. According to statistics, since the 1980s the state has allocated more than 300 million Yuan and a large amount of gold, silver and other materials for the maintenance and protection of the monasteries in Tibet. For instance, the state allocated more than 55 million Yuan for the repair of the Potala Palace, and the renovation lasted more than five years, being the largest project and involving the largest amount of capital in the maintenance history of the palace in the past few centuries. At present, Tibet has 1,787 monasteries and sites for religious activities, and over 46,000 resident monks and nuns; the region's various important religious festivals and activities are held normally; and every year more than one million Tibetan people go to Lhasa to pay homage. While maintaining the traditional Tibetan ways and styles of costume, diet and housing, the Tibetan people have absorbed many new modern civilized customs in the aspects of clothing, food, housing and transportation, as well as marriage and funerals, thus greatly enriching their lives.

—Large-scale development and construction will be certain to bring enormous pressure to bear on the fragile ecological environment of Tibet. Since the initiation of the policy of reform and opening-up, the Central Government and the local government of Tibet have consistently adhered to the strategy of sustainable development, simultaneously planning and implementing environmental protection and economic construction as an integrated process. These strategies were implemented to ensure the demonstration, design, construction and operation of engineering projects would give full consideration to eco-environmental protection to promote coordinated environmental and economic development.

The "Regulations on Environmental Protection" and the "Regulations on the Administration of Geological and Mineral Resources" have been formulated and implemented in Tibet, to form a complete system together with such state laws as the "Agrarian Management Law," " Water Law," "Law on Water and Soil Conservation," "Grassland Law" and "Law on the Protection of Wildlife." Now, with the introduction of an effective supervision and management system for environmental protection and pollution control, most of the forests, rivers, lakes, pastures, wetlands, glaciers, snow mountains and wild animals and plants in the region are well protected, and the water, air and environmental quality is excellent. Eighteen nature reserves at the national and provincial levels have been established, including those in Changtang, Mount Qomolangma and the Yarlungzangbo Grand Canyon, whose combined area accounts for half of the total area of China's nature reserves, playing an important role in the protection and improvement of the fragile plateau eco-environment.

Over the past few years, Tibet has invested over 50 million Yuan in the control of waste water and gas at enterprises and institutions such as the Lhasa Brewery, Yangbajain Power Plant, Lhasa Leather Plant, People's Hospital of the Region and Lhasa Cement Plant, effectively improving the urban environment and the quality of the region's water. Since 1991, Tibet has invested a total of 900 million Yuan in carrying out the development projects in the areas of the Yarlungzangbo, Lhasa and Nyangqu rivers, playing an active role in the prevention and control of soil erosion and the halting of desertification through the construction of water conservancy works, the improvement of pastures, the amelioration of medium- and low-yield fields, and large-scale afforestation, achieving remarkable comprehensive benefits for coordinated social, economic and environmental development.

According to the environmental evaluation indices, Tibet's ecology, which basically remains in its primordial condition, is the best in China in terms of environmental conditions. With the implementation of the state's strategy of large-scale development of the western region and the carrying out of the essential points of the Fourth Forum of the Central Government on Work in Tibet, the region is strengthening its eco-environmental protection and planning to invest 22.7 billion Yuan and launch 160 key projects for ecological protection by the mid-21st century to further protect and improve its ecological environment.

—Currently, of all the officials in Tibet, 79.4 percent are Tibetans and people from other ethnic minorities. Of the deputies to the people's congress at the regional, county and township levels, those from the Tibetan ethnic group and other ethnic minorities make up 82.4 percent, 92.62 percent and 99 percent, respectively.

- **Hu Jintao's role**

Different from all previous Chinese leaders, Hu Jintao is the first person who actually worked in Tibet, knows the people, and understands the situation in Tibet better than most people. During his term in Tibet, as the Secretary of the CPC Tibet Regional Committee since 1988, Hu Jintao has diligently worked on many areas to improve the living standard in Tibet. He even worked on the Tibet issues after he returned to Beijing. The primary areas he worked on were:

—Industry development. Hu Jintao emphasized the importance of the industry base in Tibet. Energy, light industry, textiles, machine building, pharmaceuticals, printing and several other industrial sectors progressed rapidly during his term.

—The regional market development. During Hu Jintao's term, a great number of farmers and herdsmen became businessmen, throwing themselves into the mainstream of the market economy. During his visit in July, 2001, Hu Jintao visited one of the farmer's family gave them a television as a gift to encourage them to further enhance their family's earnings and improve their living standards.

—Education and research. Hu Jintao encouraged educational and research efforts in Tibet. More schools and research institutions were established, more teachers were hired, and more Tibetans graduated from college during his term. He also facilitated to allocate more resources into schools to upgrade and purchase computers, instruction materials, and teaching equipments.

History presented Dalai Lama an opportunity with a Chinese leader that is knowledgeable and understands the issues. During his visit in the United Kingdom, people demonstrated on the street outside the Palace. Among them are two groups, one group welcomes him and supports him; the other group protested the Chinese government's hard-line policy toward Tibet. While he was walking, he stopped momentarily, and then he said, "I hope they know Tibet."

Neither Hu Jintao nor Dalai Lama has ruled out the possibility of candor discussion between them in the future. Hu Jintao has openly expressed that he would consider meeting with Dalai Lama under the condition that Dalai Lama is not seeking Tibet's independence.

There is a possibility that Hu Jintao and Dalai Lama will discuss Tibet issues together in the future. There are also a lot sincere efforts and courage required to make this happen. For both sides, peacefully resolve or even discuss the issues is a great step forward for the Tibetans and for the Chinese.

7

Religious freedom has always been a bitter topic between Chinese leaders and their western counterparts. During President Bush's visit in February 2002, he told students in Qinghua University that most Americans believe in God. He emphasized that religious freedom is protected in the United States and he wants Chinese leaders to protect religious activities.

Buddhism is the country's dominant religion with around 100 million adherents. There are more than 30 million Protestant worshippers by the end of 2001. Approximately 20 million people in the western part of China practice Islam. The government allows the practice of Christianity as long as it is done under state registered churches. Taoism is also practiced by a larger number of people.

Christianity and many other western religions have gained phenomenal popularity since the 1980s. In a small village in the Jiangsu Province, numbers of Christians increased almost ten fold in the last six years. A nationwide boom occurred at the same time. There are an estimated 70 million house-church members in China, according to Presbyterian *Religion Today,* September 6, 1999. Evangelistic zeal of its members spread like wildfire in the past 20 years. New Christians begin evangelizing almost immediately, and about 25,000 a day are added to the church. This trend was accelerated even faster when Hong Kong was returned back to China in 1997. Pat Bradley, a Christian from St. Louis, Mo., said, "most of the Chinese Christians had never met foreigners and they were remarkably gentle and meek, yet powerful in their presentation of the Gospel."

There are two conflicting views inside the Chinese government about western religions. On one hand, there are opponents who believe western religions are a serious threat to China's national security. They argue that throughout the history, western missionaries have betrayed the trust of Chinese people and threatened China's national security.

US Missionary Friedrick Brown, for example, helped the Eight-Power Allied Force in their invasion from Tianjin to Beijing in 1900. The Eight-Power Allied Force looted the priceless royal treasures in one of the most beautiful imperial gardens in human history—the Summer Palace, then burned it down to cover their crimes. He later wrote a book about his experiences on the trip. The first missionary to spread Protestantism to China, John Robert Morrison, from Britain, wrote a letter in 1825 to the board of directors of the East Indian Company expressed that he had sometimes risked his life to serve the interests of the company. One of the major businesses of the company was exporting opium into China. There is also evidence pointing to German missionary Karl Friedrich August Gutzlaff's participation in the drafting of the 1842 Nanjing Treaty, which forced the Qing Dynasty to cede Hong Kong to Britain.

Religious riots, conflicts, and wars have been with China and other countries since the beginning of recorded history, and they do not seem to go away in this century. Conflicts between religious groups inhabiting the same geographical area are everyday news. Cult leaders who bring their followers to mass suicides, or sexually abuse and rob them are certainly known to the American public. Since 1995, more than 130 people claimed John Geoghan fondled or raped them during the three decades he served in Boston-area parishes. Christian extremists in the United States attacked medical facilities and killed doctors because of dissenting beliefs.

Opponents believe that the majority of Chinese people are naïve and trusting, but some western religions are tightly integrated with political agendas and serve their own interest. Therefore, extra caution must in place in the governmental level to ensure national security is not in danger.

Supporters realized that some western missionaries really care about the Chinese people. They contributed to China's development and sincerely worked solely to spread God's words without any politics involved. Supporters also indicate the great things about western religions such as respecting neighbors and promoting family values, helping the poor and needy, providing food and shelter to the homeless.

Supporters also point out that traditional values are deteriorating in China along with the fast paced economic development. Introducing and supporting religions will enhance people's moral standards and unite people. Law enforcement can bring criminals into justice but not effectively prevent crimes. Therefore, it is necessary to allow God to play a role in people's lives. Christianity is not just a series of teachings; it is a way of life involving every area of one's existence and relationships within a society. Virtues such as lawfulness, loyalty, love, and morality are well worth learning.

Churches also played an active role in community building and social support. It helps people find friends and sponsors activities together. It provides help to the members in emotional, financial, and family needs. Christianity will give the Chinese people a very positive impact. Most believers are law-binding citizens. They follow the rules and regulations imposed by the government. Allowing people believe in God will not impose threat to the government's leadership.

Among ordinary people, they are split among the religion issues. Some people cannot distinguish the difference between religion and superstition. Atheists are the overwhelming majority in China. But this situation is changing, more and more people are studying and doing research on religion due to their intellectual curiosity.

Although Christianity has been in China for more than one thousand years and more people believe in Christianity than ever, Christians are still a minority of the Chinese population.

In the near future, Chinese government will continuously struggle between believers and non-believers, between law enforcement and religious freedom, between supporters and opponents, and between understanding and misconception.

8

The first reported AIDS case in China was discovered in 1985. Since then, the disease has been raging across the country. By the end of 2001, Chinese medical experts have estimated that about 600,000 people in the country are infected with the fatal illness. The increase rate is about 30 per cent annually over the last few years, according to figures from the Ministry of Health. The statistics indicate that 83 percent of HIV/AIDS carriers are men between the ages of 20 and 39. China is feeling the sting of an illness that is becoming an increasingly serious public health hazard and a social problem.

Yunnan Province in Southwest China is the worst hit region, followed by the Xinjiang Uygur Autonomous Region in the northwest and Guangxi Zhuang Autonomous Region in the south. In Guangdong, which borders Hong Kong and Macao, a total of 1,341 HIV carriers and 78 AIDS patients were detected in October 2001. Guangdong Province has the fourth largest HIV and AIDS toll in the country.

The AIDS development in China has been through three phases. The first phase, which began in 1985 and ended in 1988, was marked by a small number of AIDS cases in coastal cities, and those infected were mainly foreigners or overseas Chinese. The second phase, from 1989 to 1994, could be termed a limited epidemic. A small number of HIV infections were reported among drug users, labors returning from abroad, STD patients, and prostitutes. The third phase started from 1995, when HIV transmission spread around the country. A considerable number of HIV infections were reported among drug users and commercial plasma donors from various regions and the national figures for HIV infection quickly grew. At the same time HIV infection by sexual contact increased as well.

The rapid spread of HIV/AIDS in China reflects many other social problems.

The first issue is drug use.

Increasing drug use in Asia is accelerating the spread of HIV/AIDS along drug trafficking routes near Southwest China. The main heroin-producing region of China is near the borders of Laos, Myanmar, and Thailand. The region, also known as the Golden Triangle, now has a very high level of HIV infection due to injection drug use and needle sharing. Many drug users shared needles cleaned simply by cold water, not the recommended boiling water or bleach. Drug use has become one of the major accelerants of the HIV epidemic such as in Yunnan Province.

The second issue is casual sexual activities.

In Guangdong Province, most of the victims were drug addicts and homosexuals. Some contracted AIDS during casual sexual activities. About 90 per cent of the AIDS victims were men. A total of 939 AIDS victims, including 48 patients, were Guangdong residents. In China, same-sex marriage is not legalized and many people do not accept it.

In addition, prostitutes appeared in most major cities since the economic reform in 1980s. Unprotected sexual activities have increased dramatically. In the Northeastern city of Harbin, hundreds of prostitutes working for the bars in Daowai district alone. Many prostitutes are unaware of safe sex practice.

The third issue is blood transfusion.

The deadly disease is threatening a growing number of people through blood donation. In order to guarantee consistent supply of blood, the Chinese government has imposed an annual quota on local universities, government agencies and companies, and in rural areas households. Under this compulsory blood donation system, some impoverished farmers were lured to sell their blood to earn an income. Blood trade appeared in some poverty-stricken areas. At some local government-run blood banks, blood was often collected from several people at the same time and mixed together in a container, where the plasma was removed. The remaining blood was often given back to the donors, mixed with the blood of others, and all too often contaminated with HIV. Such procedures, plus the reuse of needles and un-sterilized equipment gave the disease an easy route to spread rapidly through the local population. Unfortunately, some blood contained the AIDS virus and led some astonishing infection incidents.

The Chinese government is in the process of phasing out the compulsory blood donation system. China will gradually replace the current system with voluntary donations. For example, Beijing's blood bank will depend entirely on volunteers in 2004 according to the Beijing Blood Donation Office. Other measures must accompany the blood donation system reform in order to eradicate risks in the blood business and the black market blood trade such as more accurate blood screening.

The number of AIDS patients and HIV carriers in China will only grow more when the country further integrates into the international community. Before a cure can be found, education and prevention should top the agenda in efforts to fight the epidemic.

Sufficient information about how the virus is transmitted should be provided to the public to raise their awareness of the disease. Ignorance of AIDS transmission has made an increasing number of people AIDS victims. AIDS education varies by regions. Some areas are better than the others. On February 20, 2002, *Legal Daily* reported Qingdao in East China's Shangdong Province, started AIDS prevention courses in universities, colleges and technical schools. The municipal government implemented a regulation that requires four hours of AIDS prevention classes during each term in local colleges and schools. However, there are still many local governments failing to implement effective AIDS education and prevention measures.

A more tolerant social atmosphere should be cultivated for AIDS patients to give them treatment earlier. At the same time, they should be educated to be responsible and stop the virus from spreading. Currently, AIDS patients often experience social exclusion, prejudice, and stigma from other people who often see HIV as a death sentence.

The cost of medical treatment in China for AIDS is too expensive for most patients. Before February 2002, the average monthly expenditure is above 10,000 yuan (US$1,204). Even in the richest costal cities, the average household income is around US $2,000. Therefore, majority of AIDS patients are unable to afford medical treatment. There was a big price cut during February 2002; patients need to pay around 2,000-3,000 yuan (US$240-361) per month with the new rate. Even with the new rate, it is still far from affordable for most Chinese patients.

Some Chinese legislators call for an AIDS-prevention law. China's top legislative body needs to devise a law to help curb the spread of AIDS, which is taking a firmer grip on the nation. "Such legislation is vital for the country's fight against the deadly disease, especially now that the high-incidence area is shifting from Africa to Asia," said Zhu Mingde, a Shanghai deputy to the Ninth National People's Congress (NPC). Zhu, along with 32 other deputies, submitted a proposal calling for the drafting of an AIDS-prevention law to the ongoing Fourth Session of the Ninth NPC, the nation's top legislative body. "It is a thorny issue worldwide and Chinese legislators should help solve the problem using the law," said Zhu, who is also director of Renji Hospital affiliated with the Shanghai Second Medical University.

AIDS is a very complicated problem. It is often intertwined with other issues such as the prevention of venereal diseases, drug taking, prostitution and the contamination of blood, Zhu said. "That's why we need a law to combine and co-ordinate the efforts of different departments, including health, public security, education and cultural management organs," he added. Zhu suggested that the proposed law should include the releasing of information, epidemic control and supervision and co-ordination of the dissemination of AIDS-prevention knowledge.

China needs to cooperate efforts with other nations in the battle against AIDS, especially in medical research and education. China also needs to work with its neighboring countries to fight drug trafficking and drug abuse. In addition, China needs to reorganize its own blood donation system around the country.

9

On the night of May 9, 1999, the China Central Television Station (CCTV) reporters who were busily covering the NATO bombing in Yugoslavia crowed the Chinese Embassy in Belgrade. A seasoned Japanese reporter commented that this was the first time he saw Chinese reporters covering the war story right in the war zone among other major news agencies such as BBC, and Reuters. A couple days earlier, a CNN report covered their Chinese counterparts and described them covering the NATO bombing in favor of Milosevic regime. China was one of the few countries strongly against US led NATO bombing in Yugoslavia. Some law makers in the US capital had expressed their concerns about China's position in the issue and the Chinese audience can only access the state controlled media which against NATO bombing.

Air raid sirens went off and the explosions began about 10 p.m. EDT, plunging the entire city into darkness. It was the second major power blackout in Belgrade since the war began. All of sudden, one bomb struck the Chinese Embassy. The building was immediately on fire. Almost at the same instance, another bomb exploded inside the building. Deadly smoke arised from the burning building and the falling debris soon covered furniture, injured reporters and embassy workers. People who worked in the ground level immediately ran out and cried for help. The stairs to the ground level were damaged and covered by choking smoke and fire. People who worked on the upper floors had to wait for rescue workers to come. When the rescue workers arrived, many people were evacuated via fire ladders from upper floors of the embassy. Yugoslav officials confirmed from the emergency rooms that one person was immediately killed and 26 others were injured.

The crisis immediately sent shock waves around the world. An emergency meeting was held among the Chinese leaders, and President Clinton started a meeting with Secretary of States and other senior advisors to assess the situation. The Chinese government demanded an emergency session of the U.N. Security Council to discuss the bombing of China's territory. The emergency session was arranged on 11:30 p.m. EDT at U.N. headquarters in New York. Since China is a permanent member of the Security Council, the strike on the embassy added a new dimension to the Yugoslav crisis. China's U.N. ambassador—Qin Huasan said in a statement "We are greatly shocked. NATO's barbarian act is a gross violation of the U.N. charter and international law and laws governing international relations."

Millions of television audiences in China turned on their televisions and watched the Vice President Hu Jintao gave an official speech about the embassy bombing. Hu Jintao said NATO should be held responsible for the consequences of the bombing, and called on NATO to stop its military actions immediately, so as to avoid further humanitarian disaster (see Hu Jintao's full text speech). This was the first time the United States and many other countries had a full view of Hu Jintao's appearance. His strong words prompted some western analysts prematurely labeled him as a hardliner.

Large scales of anti-American demonstrations were organized around all the American Embassy and Consulates in China: Beijing, Guangzhou, Shanghai, Shenyang and Chengdu. Some students threw tomatoes and small rocks toward the US Embassy in Beijing. Some of the front windows were shattered. Demonstrators besieged the U.S. Embassy in Beijing for four days. The Embassy employees were trapped inside the Embassy. They were frantically destroying classified documents. The ambassador along with many others had to eat canned food such as sardines and green beans for sustenance. A nightmare happened in Chengdu where some American properties caught on fire and burnt.

The U.S. State Department swiftly issued a safety advisory for U.S. citizens and business representatives traveling to China:

"Following the accidental bombing of the People's Republic of China's embassy in Belgrade by NATO-coalition forces, there have been on-going, large-scale demonstrations, incidents of harassment of private Americans and damage to U.S. businesses in the PRC.

Conditions remain volatile as a result of the extremely high anti-NATO and anti-American sentiment, and the potential exists for further demonstrations and reactions against American citizens and interests.

Circumstances in Hong Kong are relatively quiet, but the possibility of further demonstrations cannot be excluded.

The Department of State strongly urges American citizens to defer travel to the PRC until the situation stabilizes.

U.S. citizens in the PRC should remain in or very close to their homes or hotels, review their security practices, stay alert to the changing situation, and avoid crowds and demonstrations.

Airports remain open and Americans wishing to leave should be able to do so.

Official travel by U.S. government employees to the PRC has been temporarily suspended and all official U.S. government personnel in the PRC have been instructed to remain at home until the situation calms.

The U.S. Embassy in Beijing and the US consulates general in Guangzhou, Shanghai, Shenyang and Chengdu will be closed on Monday, May 10 and Tuesday, May 11, and similar action may be taken in the future as necessary.

The U.S. consulate general in Hong Kong is scheduled to remain open May 10 and May 11.

American citizens seeking emergency assistance while the embassy and consulates general are closed may not be able to reach these offices by telephone.

In such an event, they may contact the Department of State at 202-667-0900. Persons with business to conduct at the embassy or one of the consulates are advised to check in advance.

For further information on travel to the PRC, please consult the Department of State's latest consular information sheet for the People's Republic of China.

This travel warning supercedes the May 8 public announcement on the People's Republic of China, to update the current security situation, to urge Americans to defer travel to the PRC, and to reflect the temporary suspension of travel to the PRC by U.S. government employees."

A few U.S. businesses in China closed their offices that week. Many scheduled business, educational, and cultural exchange trips were immediately postponed or canceled after the State Department warning such as by the Boston Symphony Orchestra and blues musician Robert Cray.

Before the bombing of the Chinese Embassy in Belgrade, Americans were welcomed in China. Many people regard the United States, as a country China should learn from in many areas including business and technology. American cultural was prevalent in China. You can see American movies in the movie theaters, listen to the current American songs on the radio, and eat in an American restaurant chain. The college students fervently admired President Clinton when he was visiting China before the Embassy bombing.

After the bombing of the Chinese Embassy in Belgrade, anti-Western sentiment along with patriotic movement again gained its popularity. From the sacking of the emperor's residence in Beijing by European troops in the 1860s to the draconian suppression of the anti-Western Boxer Rebellion by U.S. and British-led troops in 1900, the historical grievances is still clearly remembered by many people. A student in a demonstration said, "when western powers unite to bully China, it's always the same. They are afraid of China and want to keep us down. This is just like a slap on your face then apologizes. After all, this is 1999 not 1899. Western nations can not suppress the Chinese people anymore."

In China, the bombing of Chinese Embassy in Belgrade marked a turning point in US-China relations. For hardliners in the China Communist Party (CPC), the bombing of Chinese Embassy in Belgrade confirmed their perceptions of the hostile nature of the American government against China. They believe the influence from America will soon penetrate every part of China and China will lose its own cultural, heritage, and identity. They ordered movie theaters to withdraw American movies including "Enemy of the State." The reformists in the CPC argued, politics should not mix with business. As part of the economic stability, China should not let this incident to hurt business and investments opportunities.

China refused to accept NATO's explanation of the cause of the bombing of the Chinese Embassy in Belgrade. NATO said faulty intelligence led to pilots to attack the building, believing it to be a Yugoslav military supply office. But the Chinese government questioned the validity of faulty intelligence. One of the reports on CCTV said NATO had been collecting intelligence long before the bombing campaign started. The Chinese Embassy moved to the new location about four years ago. How could CIA have such an out-dated map to direct their air campaign?

During Hu Jintao's televised speech, a special jet was on its way to Belgrade. Two men and a woman were dead in the bombing. When the special jet landed in Beijing, Vice President Hu Jintao met the jet carrying the remains of three journalists and the most seriously wounded survivors. The funeral was conducted at the highest national level—all senior Chinese leaders were present. The three journalists were then buried at Beijing's Babaoshan cemetery—resting place of many of China's revolutionary heroes.

US-China relations is one of the most volatile and complicated international issues among Hu Jintao's foreign affairs. The objective of US-China relation has always been the maintenance of peace and stability. This objective must be achieved based on frank reciprocity and of mutual respect. Unfortunately, each change of administration in the White House, results in minor policy shifts and a period of instability.

Before President George W. Bush was elected into the White House, China already worried about his support to Taiwan. The other presidential candidate Al Gore on the other hand, has demonstrated the consistent policy from President Clinton's era on the Taiwan issue. It was almost expected that President Bush's policy would cause immediate resistance from the Chinese leaders.

On April 1, 2001, an American spy plane collided with a Chinese fighter jet, and then landed on China's Hainan Island. After more than a week of intensive search in the South China Sea, the Chinese pilot Wang Wei, was presumed dead. To many western analysts' surprise, President Jiang Zemin did not delay his trip to South America for this incident. He left shortly afterward and left Hu Jintao to handle the situation. Immediately after the incident, President Bush called for China's prompt return of the airplane and the crew. While in South America, President Jiang Zemin demanded an apology from the United States for entering China's airspace without permission. President Jiang used the following analogy—"if two people bumped into each other on the street, it is expected to say 'I am sorry'. Same norm applies for two countries."

Without seeing China return the spy plane and the crew for days, some analysts believed President Bush's initial words were too strong. Some suggested President Bush should place a phone call to President Jiang Zemin, while others believe that will raise the issue into unnecessarily higher level. At the same time, the White House had almost no experience working with Hu Jintao. At one time, all the channels seem closed. Although US diplomats visited their crews in Hainan and assured the American public that their conditions are well, some democrats criticized the ineffectiveness of handling the incident and called to replace the diplomats there. The media labeled the incident as President Bush's first "foreign policy test." At the mean time, the Bush administration assessed the US-China relation in several different angles. The crews were released after the US Ambassador issued a letter to the Chinese government indicating that the United States expressed regret for the missing Chinese pilot and were "very sorry" for entering China's airspace without permission. After thirteen days, the standoff finally ended.

Since then, the seemingly shaky US-China relations have taken an upward swing. China shows support for President Bush's war on terrorism. President Bush visited Shanghai for the APEC summit. Then Bush visited Beijing in February met with President Jiang Zemin and Vice President Hu Jintao. Bush even visited the Qinghua University with Hu Jintao. Bush delivered a speech and answered some questions from the students. Hu Jintao introduced President Bush by addressing the importance of US-China relations and encouraged younger generations to learn from other countries including the United States. At the time this happened, Hu Jintao's daughter was studying in the United States under an assumed name. It is clear that Hu Jintao is open minded for learning from other countries.

There are still major sources of tension in the US-China relationship. President Bush has publicly and privately raised concerns over human rights and religious freedom, military proliferation, and Taiwan. But he also praised China's decision to press ahead with entrance into the World Trade Organization and thanked President Jiang Zemin for sharing intelligence and other cooperation in the ongoing war on terrorism.

Religious freedom was the first issue President Bush addressed with the students in Qinghua University. Prior to President Bush's visit, China released the Bible smuggler—a businessman from Hong Kong in

Fujian Province. Mr. Lam smuggled thousands Bibles to an unregistered Christian congregation in Fujian Province called "South China Church" via an unauthorized channel. In China, the authority must approve large shipment of Bibles and other religious materials.

Military proliferation is the second issue President Bush has made little progress on with his Chinese counterparts. In January 2002, the U.S. government imposed sanctions on two Chinese companies it said were supplying Iran with materials for weapons of mass destruction. China said the sanctions were unfair and must be lifted.

U.S. arms sales to Taiwan have always been a sore spot from Beijing's perspective. President Bush left open the possibility that Washington could sell Taipei warships equipped with the Aegis advanced air-defense system if China continues its military buildup across the Taiwan Straits. Although President Bush has stressed his reliance on the "one China" policy, he also made it clear that he will make calculations and decisions to balance the military capabilities on both sides of the Taiwan Strait.

China and Taiwan split amid civil war in 1949, but Beijing still regards the island as part of its territory. China has established diplomatic ties with the majority of countries and has insisted on the "one China" policy. Countries have diplomatic ties with China recognized Taiwan has one of China's province. Despite its years of effort in striving for international recognition, only less than a dozen countries have direct diplomatic ties with Taiwan. Those countries have no diplomatic ties with China.

The current ruling party in Taiwan is the Democratic Progressive Party. The public elected President is Chen Shuibian. Chen made several pro-independence speeches before and after his election. During his interview with Voice of America, Chen denied he is a Chinese.

Therefore, the Chinese leaders distrust him and have largely ignored Chen and the Democratic Progressive Party in the past.

The fast economic development and abundant labor supply in China have attracted more and more of Taiwan's businesses to invest in China. In the meantime, the Taiwan government is under intense pressure to pull Taiwan's economy out of its first recession in decades. The unemployment rate is at its highest in many years. Large scale of demonstrations occurred during 2001 in Taipei. Their economic success could determine whether President Chen Shuibian is re-elected in 2004. Under the pressure from the business community, Taiwan's government has lifted several restrictions in the recent years. China also encouraged investment from Taiwan by providing tax breaks and favorable regulations for Taiwan's investors. The first direct freight between China's Xiamen to Taiwan's Jinmen was officially opened in February 2002. Taiwan has been one of the largest investors in China. China also approved several Taiwan airlines to fly over its airspace to avoid the ongoing war on terrorism for some flights to Europe.

With stronger economic ties and more personnel exchanges in the last several years, the political front also seems to be easing its tension. During a speech in January 2002, Chinese Vice Premier Qian Qichen differentiated between what he characterized as most DPP members and those he said who seek independence for Taiwan. Qian said, "We believe there is a difference between the majority of Democratic Progressive Party members and the extremely small number of die-hard 'Taiwan independence' elements. We welcome them, under an appropriate status, to come and look around and to pay visits to further understanding." Qian's groundbreaking remarks were immediately welcomed by many people in Taiwan and sent the Taiwan's stock market up.

The Taiwan issue will continue to be a major roadblock in the US-China relations in the future. China has threatened to use force if Taiwan declares independence. President Bush also warned the Taiwan government not to do so. The recent arm sales to Taiwan has made the island becomes a place with increasingly fragile peace.

The major foundation of US-China relationship is people from both countries. The Chinese scholars who study and visit the United States have been continuously changing China economically and politically. Many western trained scholars have played an active role in China's policy making, problem solving, bridging the technology gap, economic reform, management, and investment. The deep impact will continue in the next two or three decades. Cultural exchanges between China and the United States for the past 30 years have been regarded here as successful efforts, that create heart-to-heart dialogue between the two countries.

After President Richard Nixon ended his ice-breaking visit to China, the Chinese acrobats entered the U.S. territory in 1972. The first impressions ordinary Americans had of the Chinese people were drawn from dazzling gymnastic ability and breathtaking bicycling skills. An impressed President Nixon and the First Lady, Pat Nixon, later met with the energetic Chinese artists. In 1973, about 8,800 Chinese audiences were overwhelmed by a performance of Beethoven's masterpieces by the Philadelphia Orchestra.

The contract on cultural exchanges was among the first three official documents signed between the United States and China after both countries established official diplomatic relationship in 1979. The contract established the framework of the governmental and non-governmental cultural relationships between the two countries. A total of six executive plans also guaranteed the sound and forward-thinking development of

US-China cultural exchanges based on mutual benefit, reciprocity and equal cooperation. In the same year, Chinese and American artists joined hands for the first time on the Chinese stage, when well-known Chinese musician Liu Dehai and the Boston Symphony Orchestra performed the "Lute Concerto" for a Chinese audience including senior Chinese leader Deng Xiaoping. Ever since, US-China cultural exchanges have been on the rise, reflecting a more open China.

Today, China has embraces many ways of the west. Valentine's Day fell on the third day of the Chinese Lunar New Year in 2002 and was enthusiastically welcomed alongside the age-old holiday routine. Couples strolling through the streets carried roses and chocolates in addition to the ubiquitous candied kabobs available from sidewalk vendors. Visitors to art galleries could see exhibitions of Picasso's block prints or Chinese poet Li Bai's poems and Spring Festival couplets. Young people passed on traditional New Year's greetings via cell phones. In fact, tens of millions of short messages have almost paralyzed local mobile phone grids in some areas. In many of the red envelopes stuffed with New Year's cash for unmarried people were the newly circulated euro notes.

Western-style restaurants were in holiday mode with traditional costumes for servers, and red tassels and lanterns hanging for diners to enjoy. Paper-cuts have been put up in Kentucky Fried Chicken and McDonald's, and Motorola and Coca Cola have launched new advertisements making reference to the Lunar New Year. At the annual gala New Year's Eve concert sponsored by Central China Television, a performance was held to demonstrate the Chinese people's eagerness to learn English. To prepare for the 2008 Olympic Games in Beijing, many residents have spent astonishing amount of money learning English.

The development of the international situation has repeatedly demonstrated that China and the United States shoulder important responsibilities and have extensive common interests in safeguarding peace and stability in the Asia-Pacific region and the world as a whole. Both countries are promoting regional and global economic growth and prosperity, fighting against terrorism and other cross-border crimes, and addressing environmental deterioration and other global problems. US-China friendship conforms to the wish of the people of the two countries and the trend of the times. As long as the two sides respect each other, treat each other as equals, seek common ground while reserving differences, US-China relations will be able to develop in a healthy and smooth way, he said.

Despite the political differences, the economic and culture ties between the United States and China is getting stronger and stronger. This irreversible trend will continue to be the solid foundation for mutual understanding between the two nations. People are the greatest resources that push both countries forward under united strength.

Hu Jintao's Televised Speech on Embassy Bombing

Source: Xinhua News Agency

Full Text:

Comrades, friends: Early on the morning of May 8 (Beijing time), US-led NATO wantonly used missiles to attack the Chinese embassy in the Federal Republic of Yugoslavia, causing casualties and leaving the embassy buildings devastated.

The criminal act, which is in violation of the international laws and norms of international relations, has aroused the utmost indignation of the Chinese people.

The Chinese Government on the same morning issued a solemn statement to sternly condemn the brutal act of NATO headed by the United States and demand that NATO bears all responsibilities arising from this incident.

Under the CPC Central Committee's decision, the Foreign Ministry urgently summoned US ambassador to China and issued the strongest protest.

Also, we called on the UN Security Council to convene an emergency meeting to discuss and condemn the barbarous act of US-led NATO.

We have taken all possible measures to rescue the wounded and have sent a special plane to Belgrade to take back all our relevant staff.

In the statement, our government also solemnly stated to reserve right for taking further actions.

All these measures demonstrate the common aspirations of the entire Chinese people to safeguard state sovereignty, uphold justice and oppose aggression.

On this occasion, I, on behalf of CPC Central Committee, the Chinese Government and the Chinese people, would like to express sincere regards to all staff in our embassy in Yugoslavia, extend the most profound condolences on the death of the martyrs, and convey our cordial sympathy to their relatives and to the wounded personnel.

The Chinese Government on the same morning issued a solemn statement to sternly condemn the brutal act of NATO headed by the United States and demand that NATO bears all responsibilities arising therefrom.

Under the CPC Central Committee's decision, the Foreign Ministry urgently summoned US ambassador to China and issued the strongest protest.

Also, we called on the UN Security Council to convene an emergency meeting to discuss and condemn the barbarous act of US-led NATO.

We have taken all possible measures to rescue the wounded and have sent a special plane to Belgrade to take back all our relevant staff.

In the statement, our government also solemnly stated to reserve right for taking further actions.

All these measures demonstrate the common aspirations of the entire Chinese people to safeguard state sovereignty, uphold justice and oppose aggression.

On this occasion, I, on behalf of CPC Central Committee, the Chinese Government and the Chinese people, would like to express sincere regards to all staff in our embassy in Yugoslavia, extend the most profound condolences on the death of the martyrs, and convey our cordial sympathy to their relatives and to the wounded personnel.

The Chinese Government unswervingly upholds the independent foreign policy of peace, firmly safeguards state sovereignty and national dignity and resolutely oppose hegemony and power politics.

We will uphold the policy of reform and opening to the outside world.

We will protect, in accordance with relevant international laws and norms of international relations as well as relevant laws of China, foreign diplomatic organs and personnel, foreign nationals in China and those who have come to China to engage in trade, economic, educational and cultural undertakings, and reflect the civilization and fine traditions of the Chinese nation.

The Chinese people are people who uphold justice and love peace.

We are willing, together with the people of other countries across the world, to support each other and strengthen cooperation, and work in concerted efforts for mankind's great cause of peace and development.

Let us unite closely around the Central Committee of the Communist Party of China with Comrade Jiang Zemin at the core, hold high the great banner of Deng Xiaoping Theory, be inspired with enthusiasm, and work with concerted efforts to push forward into the 21st century the great cause of building socialism with Chinese characteristics.

Appendix I

Hu Jintao's Profile
(until the end of 2001)

1942 Born in Jixi County, Anhui Province

1965 Graduated from Qinghua University in Beijing

1968 Technician of the Gansu Ministry of Water Resources and Electric Power engineering bureau

1974 Secretary of the Gansu Provincial Construction Committee

1975 Deputy chief of the Gansu Provincial Construction Committee designing management division

1980 Deputy director of the Gansu Provincial Construction Committee

1980 Secretary of the Gansu Provincial Committee of the Chinese Communist Youth League(CCYL)

1982 Member of the Secretariat of the CCYL Central Committee and president of the All-China Youth Federation

1984 The first secretary of the Secretariat of the Central Committee of the Chinese Communist Youth League

1985 Secretary of the Communist Party of China (CPC) Guizhou Provincial Committee

1988 Secretary of the CPC Tibet Autonomous Regional Committee

1992 Standing Committee member of the Political Bureau of the CPC Central Committee member of the Central Committee's Secretariat

1993 President of the Party School of the CPC Central Committee

1998 State Vice President

1999 Vice chairman of the PRC Central Military Commission

Appendix II

The Structure of PRC Government

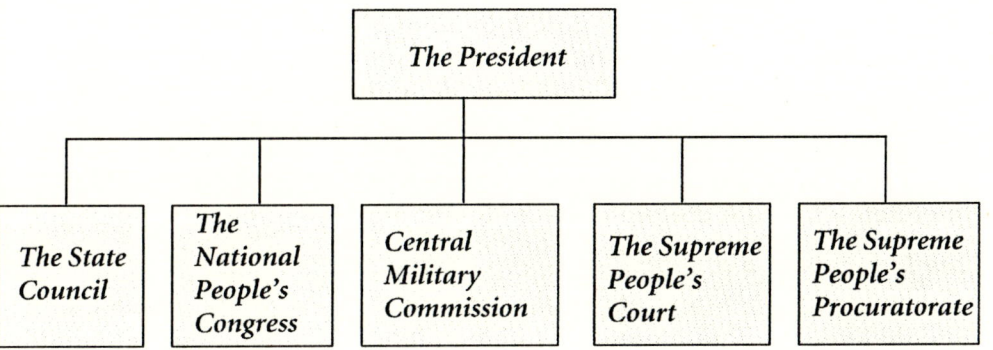

The President

The president and vice president are elected by the National People's Congress. The term of office of the president and vice president is five years, no more than two five year terms can be served consecutively. Both the president and vice president receive heads of state at home and travel abroad representing China.

The president, in accordance with decisions taken by the National People's Congress appoints and removes the premier, the vice premiers, state councilors, ministers, and other high ranking officials. The vice president assists in the presidential work and in the event the office of the president falls vacant, succeeds to the position of president.

Executive branch: The State Council

The State Council is the executive body of the Chinese government. The State Council formulate rules, makes policy decisions and coordinates the work of the various state organs. It is responsible for the day-to-day administration of the country. It formulates the tasks and responsibilities of the ministries and the commissions, supervises the provincial and local government administration bodies and directs and administers the affairs of everything from education, culture, public health and family planning to civil affairs, judicial matters and public security.

Flowing from the State Council are 22 ministries. These ministries are vertical structures responsible for one particular field of activities.

- Ministry of Foreign Affairs
- Ministry of National Defense
- Ministry of Education
- Ministry of Science and Technology
- Ministry of Public Security
- Ministry of State Security
- Ministry of Supervision
- Ministry of Civil Affairs
- Ministry of Justice
- Ministry of Finance
- Ministry of Personnel
- Ministry of Labor and Social Security
- Ministry of Land and Natural Resources

- Ministry of Construction
- Ministry of Railways
- Ministry of Communications
- Ministry of Information Industry
- Ministry of Water Resources
- Ministry of Agriculture
- Ministry of Foreign Trade and Economic Cooperation
- Ministry of Culture
- Ministry of Health

Flowing from the State Council are 10 State Commissions. These state-level commissions are the first tier organizations under, and reporting to, the State Council. These state commissions act similar to the ministries and have similar authority, but tend to play a more supervisory and policy-setting role. They are staffed by a president and up to 10 vice presidents.

- State Planning Commission
- State Economic and Trade Commission
- State Commission for Restructuring the Economic Systems
- State Education Commission
- State Science and Technology Commission
- National Defense Commission for Science, Technology and Industry
- State Nationalities Affairs Commission
- China State Physical Culture and Sports Commission
- State Family Planning Commission
- People's Bank of China

Under the direct leadership of the State Council are 13 bureaus, seven administrative offices, eight institutions, 15 bureaus and 14 state-level companies and corporations. These various bodies are independent of the ministries and commissions. Some have a limited life, such as the commission overseeing the planning and construction of the Three Gorges Dam project on the Yangtze river.

Legislative branch: National People's Congress

The National People's Congress, or parliament, is the highest legislation-making body in China. It approves or rejects suggestions issued by the State Council, including the election of state president and vice president and other high-ranking politicians. Upon the appropriate nominations, the National People's Congress holds the authority to choose the premier and chairman of the Central Military Commission, two very important positions in China. Power to amend, enforce and supervise the constitution rests with the national congress. It also approves national economic and social plans and passes the state budget.

The congress is comprised of 3,000 deputies, representing China's 30 provinces, autonomous regions and municipalities. Representatives of the armed forces are also selected to be deputies in the National People's Congress. Deputies take office for a five year term. The National People's Congress meets for about two to three weeks, usually in February or March. The congress to meet at least once annually, and supervise ministries, commissions and other government branches.

Military branch: Central Military Commission

The Central Military Commission is the highest policy-making body of the People's Liberation Army, and the country's top military command body. The commission is headed by a chairman. The Chairman is responsible to the National People's Congress and its Standing Committee.

Although China has a Defense Ministry, the real and important defense decisions are made at the Central Military Commission. This commission has the authority to pass along resolutions to the Defense Ministry for implementation. The Central Military Commission is expected to include representation from special forces commanders — navy, air force and missile troops — and all seven of China's major military zones.

Judiciary branch: The Supreme People's Court

The Supreme People's Court is the highest judicial body in China. It reports to the National People's Congress and is responsible for advising provincial and municipal courts, and handles those cases which extend beyond a single province or members of state bodies. All cases are open to the public with exceptions of the cases involved in national security, personal privacy, and minors.

Procuratorial branch: The Supreme People's Procuratorate

The Supreme People's Procuratorate is the highest legal supervisory organ. It supervises the activities of the other state organs and officials, acting like the government's police department. This body is empowered to bring back in line those officials and or agencies which have strayed from the government line. It reports to the National People's Congress and its Standing Committee.

Appendix III

White Paper on Tibet's March Toward Modernization

Source: Xinhua News Agency
Date: 11/08/2001
Full Text:

The Information Office of the State Council issued Thursday a white paper on the modernization drive of Tibet. The following is the full text of the white paper entitled "Tibet's March Toward Modernization":

FOREWORD

Modernization has been an important issue confronting countries and regions worldwide in modern times. Since the invasion of the Western powers in the mid-19th century, it has been the most important task of the people of all ethnic groups in China, the Tibetan people included, to get rid of poverty and backwardness, shake off the lot of being trampled upon, and build up an independent, united, strong, democratic and civilized modern country. Since the founding of the People's Republic of China in 1949, and especially since the introduction of reform and opening to the outside world, the modernization drive in China has been burgeoning with each passing day, and achieved successes attracting worldwide attention. China is taking vigorous steps to open even wider and become more prosperous. China's Tibet, with its peaceful liberation in 1951 as the starting point, has carried out regional ethnic autonomy and made a historical leap in its social system following the Democratic Reform in 1959 and the elimination of the feudal serf system. Through carrying out socialist construction and the reform and opening-up, Tibet has made rapid progress in its modernization drive and got onto the track of development in step with the other parts of the country, revealing a bright future for its development.

This year is the 50th anniversary of the peaceful liberation of Tibet. Looking back on the course of modernization since its peaceful liberation, publicizing the achievements in modernization made by the people of all ethnic groups in Tibet through their hard work and with the support of the Central Government and the whole nation, and revealing the law of development of Tibet's modernization-these will contribute not only to accelerating the healthy development of Tibet's modernization but also to clearing up various misunderstandings on the "Tibet issue" in the international community and promoting overall understanding of the past and present situations in Tibet.

I. THE RAPID SOCIAL DEVELOPMENT IN TIBET

Modernization has been the fundamental question in the social development of Tibet in modern times. The feudal serfdom under theocracy, which had lasted for several hundred years in Tibet, became an extremely decadent social system that contradicted the progressive trend in the modern world, for it stifled the development of the social productive forces of Tibet, seriously hindered social progress, relegated Tibet to the state of extreme poverty, backwardness, isolation and decline, to the point verging on total collapse.

> ➢ BACKWARD SOCIAL SYSTEM AND HARSH ECONOMIC EXPLOITATION.

The society of old Tibet under feudal serfdom was even more dark and backward than in Europe in the Middle Ages. The three major estate- holders + officials, nobles and upper-ranking monks in monasteries + accounted for less than five percent of Tibet's total population but owned all the farmland, pastures, forests, mountains and rivers, and the majority of the livestock. The serfs and slaves, accounting for more than 95 percent of the population, owned no land or other means of production. They had no personal freedom, had to depend totally on the manors of estate-holders for livelihood or act as their family slaves from generation to generation. They were subjected to the three-fold exploitation of corvee labor, taxes and high-interest loans and their lives were no more than struggles for existence. According to incomplete statistics, there were over 200 kinds of taxes levied by the Kasha (the former local government of Tibet) alone. Slaves had to contribute more than 50 percent or even 70 to 80 percent of their labor free to the Kasha and estate-holders, and over 60 percent of the farmers and herdsmen were burdened with similar high-interest loans.

> RIGID HIERARCHY AND SAVAGE POLITICAL OPPRESSION.

The "13-Article Code" and "16-Article Code" of old Tibet divided the people into three classes and nine ranks, enshrining social and political inequality between the different ranks in law. These codes explicitly stated that the life of a person of the highest rank of the upper class was literally worth his weight in gold, while that of a person of the lowest rank of the lower class was worth only the price of a straw rope. Serfs could be sold, transferred, given away, mortgaged or exchanged by their owners, who had the power over their births, deaths and marriages. Male or female serfs belonging to different owners had to pay a "redemption fee" if they wished to marry, and their children were doomed to be serfs for life. Serf-owners could punish their serfs at will. The punishments included flogging, cutting off their hands or feet, gouging out their eyes, chopping off their ears or tongues, pulling out their tendons, drowning them and throwing them down from cliffs.

> THEOCRACY AND THE FETTERS OF RELIGION.

Religion and monasteries "commanded the highest respect" in old Tibet with its theocratic socio-political structure. As the sole ideology and an independent politico-economic entity, they enjoyed immense influence and numerous political and economic privileges and had control over people's spiritual life. The upper-class monks and priests were Tibet's principal political rulers and also the biggest serf-owners. The Dalai Lama, as one of the heads of the Gelug Sect of Tibetan Buddhism and concurrently the leader of the local government of Tibet, had all the political and religious powers in his hands. The former local government of Tibet practiced a dual clerical and secular officials system, in which the monk officials were senior to the lay officials. According to the 1959 statistics, of the 3.3 million kai (unit of measurement for area used by the Tibetan people, 1 kai;1/15 hectare) of cultivated land in Tibet, 1.2144 million kai were owned by monasteries and upper-class monks, accounting for 36.8 percent of the total cultivated land, while aristocrats and clerical and secular officials owned 24 percent and 38.9 percent, respectively. The Drepung Monastery owned 185 manors, 20,000 serfs, 300 pastures and 16,000 herdsmen. According to a survey conducted in the 1950s, Tibet had more than 2,700 temples and monasteries and 120,000 monks, or 12 percent of the total population in Tibet, and about one-fourth of the male population were monks. In 1952, Lhasa had an urban population of 37,000, of whom 16,000 were monks. The widespread temples, numerous monks and frequent religious activities consumed a huge amount of manpower and the greater part of material wealth in Tibet, greatly hindering the development of the productive forces there. According to the American Tibetologist Melvyn C. Goldstein, religion and the monasteries were "extremely conservative" and "played a major role in thwarting progress" in Tibet;

"This commitment...to the universality of religion as the core metaphor of Tibetan national identity will be seen...to be a major factor underlying Tibet's inability to adapt to changing circumstances."

> ➤ LOW LEVEL OF DEVELOPMENT AND A PRECARIOUS LIFE.

Cruel oppression and exploitation by the feudal serf-owners, and especially the endless consumption of human and material resources by religion and monasteries under the theocratic system and their spiritual enslavement of the people, had gravely damped the laborers' enthusiasm for production, stifled the vitality of the Tibetan society and reduced Tibet to a protracted state of stagnancy. Even in the middle of the 20th century, Tibet was still extremely isolated and backward, almost without a trace of modern industry, commerce, science and technology, education, culture and health care; primitive farming methods were still being used; and herdsmen had to travel from place to place grazing their livestock. There were few strains and breeds of grains and animals, and some of them had even degenerated. Farm tools were primitive, grain yield was only 4 to 10 times the seeds sown, and the level of both the productive forces and social development was very low. Deaths from hunger and cold, poverty and diseases were commonplace among the serfs, and the streets in Lhasa, Xigaze, Qamdo and Nagqu were crowded with beggars of both sexes, young and old.

Imperialist invasion brought more disasters for the Tibetan people, and deepened the social contradictions in Tibet, making it go from bad to worse. From the middle of the 19th century, China became a semi-colonial and semi-feudal country, and Tibet, just like most other parts of the country, was invaded by the Western powers. In their invasions of Tibet British imperialists made no scruple about burning, killing and looting, secured many privileges through a number of unequal treaties, and carried out colonialist control and exploitation by wantonly plundering Tibet' s resources and dumping their goods on the Tibetan people. At the same time, they fostered their trusted followers from among the ruling class and groomed their agents, in an attempt to divide Tibet from China. Weighed down by the internal and external double oppression and exploitation, the masses of the serfs fared worse and worse, driving them constantly to present petitions to the government, flee from the land, refuse to pay rent or offer corvee service and even raise armed revolts. Danger lurked on every side in Tibet and "the theocratic system is declining like a lamp consuming its last drop of oil."2 Ngapoi Ngawang Jigme, once a Kaloon (council minister) of the former local government of Tibet, pointed out in the 1940s several times that if Tibet "goes on like this, the serfs will all die in the near future, and the nobles will not be able to live either. The whole Tibet will be destroyed. "3 So there was a historically imperative need for the progress of Tibetan society and the happiness of the Tibetan people to expel the imperialists and shake off the yoke of feudal serfdom.

The founding of the People's Republic of China in 1949 brought hope for the deeply distressed Tibetan people. In conforming to the law of historical development and the interests of the Tibetan people, the Central People's Government worked actively to bring about Tibet's peaceful liberation. After that, important policies and measures were adopted for Tibet's Democratic Reform, regional autonomy, large-scale modernization and reform and opening-up. All this has contributed to changing the lot of Tibet and propelling Tibetan society forward in seven-league boots.

> ➢ THE PEACEFUL LIBERATION OPENED THE WAY FOR TIBET TO MARCH TOWARD MODERNIZATION.

On May 23, 1951 the "Agreement on Measures for the Peaceful Liberation of Tibet" (hereinafter referred to as the "17-Article Agreement") was signed by the Central People's Government and the local government of Tibet, marking the realization of the peaceful liberation of Tibet and opening a new page for the development of the region. The peaceful liberation of Tibet, which was a part of China's national democratic revolution, enabled Tibet to shake off the penetration of imperialist forces and the political and economic shackles imposed by them, ended the discrimination and oppression against the Tibetan ethnic group in old China, safeguarded the national sovereignty, unification and territorial integrity of China, realized the unity of all ethnic groups in China and the internal unity of Tibet, and created the essential prerequisites for Tibet to join the other parts of the country in the drive for common progress and development. After the peaceful liberation, the People's Liberation Army and people from other parts of China working in Tibet persisted in carrying out the 17-Article Agreement and the policies of the Central Government, actively helped the Tibetan people build the Xikang-Tibet and Qinghai-Tibet highways, the Damxung Airport, water conservancy projects, modern factories, banks, trading companies, post offices, farms and schools. They adopted a series of measures to help the farmers and herdsmen expand production, started social relief and disaster relief programs, and provided free medical service for the prevention and treatment of epidemic and other diseases. All this has promoted the economic, social and cultural development of Tibet, created a new social atmosphere of modern civilization and progress, produced a far-reaching influence among people of all walks of life in Tibet, ended the long-term isolation and stagnation of the Tibetan society, paved the way for Tibet's march toward a modern society, and opened up wide prospects for Tibet's further development.

> THE DEMOCRATIC REFORM CLEARED THE WAY FOR THE MODERNIZATION OF TIBET.

In 1951, when Tibet was liberated peacefully, in consideration of the special history and reality of Tibet the "17-Article Agreement" affirmed the necessity of reforming the social system of Tibet and, at the same time, adopted a prudent attitude toward the reform. It stipulated that "the local government of Tibet shall carry out reform voluntarily, and, when the people demand a reform, shall settle it through consultation with the Tibetan leaders." However, some people in the Tibetan ruling group were totally opposed to reform and raised a hue and cry about their determination never to carry it out, in order to perpetuate the feudal serf system. Faced with the Tibetan people's ever-stronger demand for a democratic reform, instead of following the popular will they ganged up with overseas anti-China forces and raised an armed rebellion on March 10, 1959, in an attempt to split Tibet from the motherland and seek "independence" for Tibet. In order to safeguard the unity of the nation and the basic interests of the Tibetan people, the Central People's Government took decisive measures to suppress the rebellion together with the Tibetan people, and carried out the Democratic Reform of the Tibetan social system.

The Democratic Reform abolished the feudal serf-owners' right to own land and the serfs and slaves' personal bondage to the feudal serf-owners, repealed the old Tibetan laws and barbarous punishments, and annulled the theocratic system and the feudal privileges of the clergy. The reform liberated Tibet's million serfs and slaves politically, economically and spiritually, making them masters of the land and other means of production, giving them personal and religious freedom, and realizing their human rights. The reform greatly liberated the social productive forces in Tibet, and opened up the road toward modernization. According to statistics, the former serfs and slaves got over 2.8 million kai of land in the Democratic Reform and, in 1960, when the Democratic Reform was basically completed, the total grain yield for the whole of Tibet was 12.6 percent higher than in 1959 and 17.7 percent higher than in 1958, before the Democratic Reform. Moreover, the total amount of livestock was 9.9 percent more than in 1959.

> THE IMPLEMENTATION OF REGIONAL ETHNIC AUTONOMY PROVIDED A FIRM INSTITUTIONAL GUARANTEE FOR THE MODERNIZATION OF TIBET.

After the Democratic Reform, the Tibetan people, like people of all other ethnic groups throughout China, enjoyed all the political rights provided by the Constitution and law. In 1961, a general election was held all over Tibet. For the first time, the former serfs and slaves were able to enjoy democratic rights as their own masters, and actively participated in the election of power organs and governments at all levels in the region. Many emancipated serfs and slaves took up leading posts at various levels in the region. In September 1965, the First People's Congress of Tibet was successfully convened, at which the founding of the Tibet Autonomous Region and the Regional People's Government was officially proclaimed. The founding of the Tibet Autonomous Region and the implementation of regional ethnic autonomy institutionally ensured the realization of the policy of equality, unity, mutual help and common prosperity among all ethnic groups in the region, and guaranteed the Tibetan people's right to equal participation in the administration of state affairs as well as the right to independent administration of local and ethnic affairs. In this way, an institutional guarantee was provided for Tibet to develop along with the other parts of China, with special support and assistance by the state and according to its local characteristics.

➢ THE POLICY OF REFORM AND OPENING-UP GAVE A POWERFUL IMPETUS TO THE MODERNIZATION OF TIBET.

The 1980s witnessed a great upsurge of the reform, opening-up and modernization drive in Tibet, as in the other parts of China. To promote the development of Tibet, the Central Government formulated a series of special favorable policies, such as "long- term right to use and independently operate land by individual households" and "long-term policy of individual households' ownership, raising and management of livestock." These policies promoted the reform of the economic system and opening-up in Tibet. Since 1984, 43 projects have been launched in Tibet with state investment and aid from nine provinces and municipalities.

The implementation of the policy of reform and opening-up and the state aid have strengthened and invigorated Tibetan industry, agriculture, animal husbandry and the tertiary industry with trade, catering and tourism as its mainstays, raised the overall level of industries and the level of commercialization of economic activities in Tibet, and helped Tibet take another step forward in its economic and social development.

> ➢ THE MODERNIZATION DRIVE IN TIBET HAS ENTERED THE NEW STAGE OF RAPID DEVELOPMENT WITH THE STRATEGIC DECISION OF THE CENTRAL GOVERNMENT TO ACCORD SPECIAL ATTENTION TO TIBET AND GET ALL THE OTHER PARTS OF CHINA TO AID TIBET.

In 1994, the Central Government held the Third Forum on Work in Tibet, and set the guiding principles for work in the region in the new era as follows: Focusing efforts on economic construction, firmly grasping the two major tasks of developing the economy and stabilizing the situation, securing the high-speed development of the economy, overall social progress and lasting political stability in Tibet, and ensuring continuous improvement of the Tibetan people's living standards. At the forum, the Central Government also adopted the important decision to devote special attention to Tibet and get all the other parts of China to aid Tibet, and formulated a sequence of special favorable policies and measures for speeding up the development of Tibet. The forum formed a mechanism for all-round aid to the modernization of Tibet, by which the state would directly invest in construction projects in the region, the Central Government provide financial subsidies, and the other parts of the country provide counterpart aid. Since 1994, the Central Government has directly invested a total of 4.86 billion yuan in 62 projects; 15 provinces and municipalities and the various ministries and commissions under the State Council have also given aid gratis for the construction of 716 projects, contributing a total of 3.16 billion yuan; and over 1,900 cadres have been sent from all over the country to assist in Tibet's construction.

As a result, the production and living conditions in Tibet have been greatly improved and its social and economic developments revved up. In the meantime, Tibet has promoted all-round reform in its economic and technological systems, adjusted its economic structure and mechanism of enterprise operation and management, set up a complete social security system, enlarged its scope of opening-up, and actively encouraged and attracted funds from both home and abroad for its economic construction. In this way, the economy with diverse forms of ownership has developed rapidly, and Tibet's inner vitality for growth has been strengthened. In June 2001, the Central Government held the Fourth Forum on Work in Tibet, at which it drew up an ambitious blueprint for Tibet's overall modernization in the new century, and decided to adopt more effective policies and measures to further strengthen the support for the modernization of Tibet.

With attention from the Central Government, aid from the other parts of the country and the efforts of people of all ethnic groups in Tibet, the development of the region's economy has been speeded up, the people's living standards have been greatly improved, and the modernization drive is vibrant with life as never before. According to statistics, from 1994 to 2000, the gross domestic product (GDP) in Tibet increased by 130 percent, or a yearly increase of 12.4 percent, changing the situation in which Tibet had lagged behind the other parts of China in the GDP growth rate for a long time in the past. Urban residents' disposable income per capita and the farmers and herdsmen's income per capita increased by 62.9 percent and 93.6 percent, respectively; and the impoverished population decreased from 480,000 in the early 1990s to just over 70,000.

To sum up, the development history of Tibet in the past five decades since its peaceful liberation has been one of proceeding from darkness to brightness, from backwardness to progress, from poverty to prosperity and from isolation to openness, and of the region marching toward modernization as a part of the big family of China.

I. TIBET'S MODERNIZATION ACHIEVEMENTS

In the past 50 years, thanks to the leadership of the Central Government, the aid of the whole nation and the unremitting efforts of the people of all ethnic groups in the region, Tibet has kept marching forward along the road to modernization and made significant achievements that have attracted worldwide attention.

> THE ECONOMY HAS PROGRESSED SIGNIFICANTLY.

During the past 50 years, Tibet has witnessed tremendous changes in its economic system and economic structure and significant progress in its aggregate economic volume. Having thoroughly eliminated the former closed, natural economy based on the manorial system, Tibet is fast on its way toward a modern market economy. In 2000, the region's GDP reached 11.746 billion yuan, twice as much as in 1995, four times as much as in 1990, and over 30 times as much as in the pre-peaceful liberation period. The economic structure is becoming more and more rational. The primary industry accounted for 30.9 percent in the GDP, as against 99 percent 50 years ago, and the proportions of the secondary and tertiary industries rose to 23.2 percent and 45.9 percent, respectively.

Modern industry, having grown from nothing, has gradually become an important pillar of the rapid economic development in Tibet. So far, over 20 branches of the industry have been set up, including energy, light industry, textiles, machine building, lumbering, mining, building materials, chemicals, pharmaceuticals, printing and foodstuff processing. This modern industrial system with Tibetan characteristics has produced some nationally famous brand names, such as Lhasa Beer, Qizheng Tibetan Medicine and Zhufeng Motorcycles. By 2000, Tibet had 482 enterprises at and above the township level and the added value of its secondary industry reached 2.721 billion yuan.

Basic industries, such as energy and transportation, have thrived. Power industry has developed rapidly, and a new energy system has been formed, with hydropower as the mainstay backed up by supplementary energy sources such as geothermal power, wind energy and solar energy. By 2000, there were 401 power plants in Tibet, with a total installed capacity of 356,200 kw and an annual energy output of 661 million kwh + a world of difference from before the peaceful liberation, when there was only one 125-kw power plant, which worked irregularly and supplied electricity only to a handful of aristocrats. Putting an end to the history of Tibet having not a single highway, a three-dimensional transportation system is now in place, with highway transportation as the major part, and air and pipeline transportation developing in coordination. A highway network now extends in all directions with Lhasa as the center, including such trunk roads as the Qinghai-Tibet, Sichuan-Tibet, Xinjiang-Tibet, Yunnan-Tibet and China-Nepal highways and 15 main highways and 375 branch highways. These roads total 22,500 km, and reach every county and over 80 percent of the townships in the region. The two civil airports in Tibet, Gonggar Airport in Lhasa and Bamda Airport in Qamdo, operate domestic and international routes from Lhasa to Beijing, Chengdu, Chongqing, Xi'an, Xining, Shanghai, Deqen and Kunming in Yunnan Province, Hong Kong, and Kathmandu of Nepal. Meanwhile, a 1,080-km petroleum pipeline has been built from Golmud in Qinghai Province to Lhasa, the highest-altitude pipeline in the world. It carries over 80 percent of petroleum transported in the region. In June 2001, work started on the Qinghai-Tibet Railway, and the days when the region was inaccessible by rail will be gone for good in the foreseeable future.

The tertiary industry has become the largest industrial sector in Tibet. Such newly emerging industries as modern commerce, tourism, postal services, catering, entertainment and information technology, unknown in old Tibet, have grown by leaps and bounds. Telecommunications have developed particularly speedily, and an advanced modern telecommunications network covering the whole of Tibet has taken shape, with Lhasa as the center, and including cable and satellite transmission together with program-controlled switching systems, digital and mobile communications. In 2000, Tibet Telecom business totaled 384 million yuan-worth and its income was 123 million yuan, 179 times and 1,086 times the 1978 figures, respectively, and on average increasing by 26.6 percent and 24.3 percent respectively each year over the past 22 years. By the end of 2000, the total installed capacity of fixed telephones reached 170,200, and 111,100 telephones were installed. The total installed capacity of mobile telephones has reached 123,000, with 72,300 mobile telephone users. There are also nine Internet websites and 4,513 users. By 2000, the added value of the tertiary industry had reached 5.393 billion yuan, the highest among all the constituents of the region's GDP.

The mode of production in agriculture and animal husbandry has changed radically, and the productive forces and production returns have risen by big margins. Since the peaceful liberation, the state has invested heavily in water conservancy works, and put great efforts into a number of capital construction projects for agriculture and animal husbandry, especially in the comprehensive development of the middle reaches of the Yarlungzangbo, Lhasa and Nyangqu rivers. These endeavors have greatly improved the agricultural and animal husbandry production conditions in Tibet, and are changing the Tibetan peasants and herdsmen's traditional lifestyles of living at the mercy of the elements. A series of agricultural and stockbreeding technologies have been spread widely, including scientific fertilization, improvement of breeds, pest control and stockraising. The mechanization of agriculture and production efficiency have both improved by a large margin, and farming and animal husbandry are advancing along the line of modernization. By 2000, the added value of the primary industry in Tibet had reached 3.632 billion yuan, the total grain yield had reached 962,200 tons, the total amount of livestock had come to 22.66 million head, self-sufficiency in grains and edible oils had been basically realized, and the distribution of meat and milk per capita had risen above the national average.

> THE LEVEL OF URBANIZATION HAS CONSTANTLY IMPROVED.

With its natural economy old Tibet lacked the dynamics of urban development and had only a few small cities and towns. Lhasa, the most populous urban center, had a population of just over 30,000. Other places with comparatively large populations were big villages rather than cities, each having only a few thousand residents. Even Lhasa lacked a sound urban operating mechanism of any sort and had scarcely any of the amenities of a proper city. At present, the urban scale of Tibet is expanding constantly together with industrial growth. By 2000, there were two organic cities in Tibet, 72 counties and districts and 112 organic towns. Moreover, the urban population totaled 491,100, and the total urban area was 147 sq m. The comprehensive functions of the cities and towns have improved steadily, and complete systems have taken shape in various fields, such as roads, water supply, public security and community services, basically satisfying the needs of the lives of the urban residents and the economic development of the cities. Tibet is now marching toward modernization in urban appearance and environmental protection. Its urban environmental index now ranks first in the country with the per capita area of its urban public lawns reaching 10.27 sq m and a greenbelt coverage of 24.4 percent. Urban development groups radiating from Lhasa have come into existence in Tibet, while efforts are being made to form an economic pattern centered on cities and towns to promote economic development in neighboring areas and stimulate mutual development through the integration of urban and rural areas.

> REMARKABLE ACHIEVEMENTS HAVE BEEN MADE IN OPENING UP.

The policy of reform and opening-up has promoted the unprecedented development of Tibet's commerce, foreign trade and tourism, and strengthened its interrelations and cooperation with the inland areas and the rest of the world. The regional market system has taken initial shape, and is gradually being integrated into the market system of the whole country and even that of the world. A great number of farmers and herdsmen have become businessmen, throwing themselves into the mainstream of the market economy. Commodities from other parts of the country and the world are flowing into Tibet in a continuous stream to enrich both the urban and rural markets and the lives of the local people. A great quantity of Tibetan famous-brand products, and special local products and handicrafts have entered the domestic and international markets. The flourishing of commerce and trade has given a powerful impetus to the development of the farm and stock-breeding products processing industry and, as a result, agriculture and animal husbandry are going market-oriented. The state has formulated a series of preferential policies to encourage domestic and foreign enterprises to invest in enterprises in Tibet, and expand both domestic and international economic exchanges and cooperation. Tibet has attained the contractual value of US$ 125 million in overseas investment over the past five years. By 2000, its total imports and exports had reached US$ 130 million-worth, of which the total export value came to US$ 113 million.

The "roof of the world" has become one of China's most popular tourist destinations, attracting numerous tourists from both home and abroad with its unique natural views and places of cultural interest. In 2000, Tibet received a total of 598,300 tourists from both home and abroad, of whom 148,900 were overseas tourists, earning a direct income of 780 million yuan, and an indirect income of 2.98 billion yuan, accounting for 6.6 percent and 25.38 percent of the region's GDP, respectively.

> ENVIRONMENTAL AND ECONOMIC DEVELOPMENT HAS PROGRESSED IN COORDINATION.

Large-scale development and construction will be certain to bring enormous pressure to bear on the fragile ecological environment of Tibet. Since the initiation of the policy of reform and opening-up, the Central Government and the local government of Tibet have consistently adhered to the strategy of sustainable development, simultaneously planning and implementing environmental protection and economic construction as an integral whole, to guarantee that the demonstration, design, construction and operation of engineering projects would give full consideration to eco-environmental protection to promote coordinated environmental and economic development. The " Regulations on Environmental Protection" and the "Regulations on the Administration of Geological and Mineral Resources" have been formulated and implemented in Tibet, to form a complete system together with such state laws as the "Agrarian Management Law," " Water Law," "Law on Water and Soil Conservation," "Grassland Law" and "Law on the Protection of Wildlife." Now, with the introduction of an effective supervision and management system for environmental protection and pollution control, most of the forests, rivers, lakes, pastures, wetlands, glaciers, snow mountains and wild animals and plants in the region are well protected, and the water, air and environmental quality is excellent. Eighteen nature reserves at the national and provincial levels have been established, including those in Changtang, Mount Qomolangma and the Yarlungzangbo Grand Canyon, whose combined area accounts for half of the total area of China's nature reserves, playing an important role in the protection and improvement of the fragile plateau eco-environment. Over the past few years, Tibet has invested over 50 million yuan in the control of waste water and gas at enterprises and institutions such as the Lhasa Brewery, Yangbajain Power Plant, Lhasa Leather Plant, People's Hospital of the Autonomous Region and Lhasa Cement Plant, effectively improving the urban environment and the quality of the region's water. Since 1991, Tibet has invested a total of 900 million yuan in carrying out the development projects in the areas of the Yarlungzangbo, Lhasa and Nyangqu rivers, playing an active role in the prevention and control of soil erosion and the halting of desertification through the construction of water conservancy works, the improvement of pastures, the amelioration of medium- and low-yield fields, and large-scale afforestation, achieving remarkable comprehensive benefits for coordinated social, economic and environmental development. According to the environmental evaluation indices, Tibet's ecology, which basically remains in its primordial condition, is the best in China in terms of environmental conditions. With the implementation of the state's strategy of large-scale development of the western region and the carrying out of the essential points of the Fourth Forum of the Central Government on Work in Tibet, the region is strengthening its eco-environmental protection and planning to invest 22.7 billion yuan and launch 160 key projects for ecological protection by the mid-21st century to further protect and improve its ecological environment.

> RAPID PROGRESS HAS BEEN MADE IN EDUCATION, SCIENCE AND TECHNOLOGY, AND MEDICAL AND HEALTH CARE.

In old Tibet there was not a single school in the modern sense, and education was monopolized by monasteries. The enrollment ratio of school-age children was less than two percent, and the illiteracy rate of the young and middle-aged people reached 95 percent. But now, education has been widely popularized, and the broad masses of the people enjoy the right to receive education. The state has invested enormously in developing education, and a complete education system is now in place, covering regular education, preschool education, adult education, vocational education and special education. By 2000, Tibet had set up 956 schools of all kinds, with a total enrollment of 381,100 students; the enrollment ratio of school-age children had increased to 85.8 percent; the illiteracy rate had declined to 32.5 percent; and 33,000 persons had received education above the junior college level, accounting for

12.6 per thousand of the region's total population and higher than the average national level. Now Tibet not only boasts its own master's and doctorate degree holders, but also a number of nationally renowned experts and scholars.

Growing out of nothing, modern science and technology have been developing rapidly. There was no modern scientific research institute in Tibet before its peaceful liberation, and even such applied technology as astronomy and calendrical calculation were monopolized by the monasteries behind a mysterious religious facade. Attaching great importance to scientific research and the popularization and application of science and technology, the Central Government and the local government of Tibet have set up 25 scientific research institutes over the past half century, employing 35,000 professional scientific and technical personnel in disciplines such as history, economics, population, linguistics and religion, and dozens of sectors such as agriculture, animal husbandry, forestry, ecology, biology, Tibetan medicine and pharmacology, salt lakes, geo-thermal and solar energy, among which studies in Tibetology, plateau ecology, Tibetan medicine and pharmacology take the lead in the country. Besides, a number of academic achievements made in Tibet are of worldwide influence.

Medical and health care has grown vigorously. In the old days, when traditional Tibetan medicine was monopolized by feudal nobles and monasteries, the region was extremely short of doctors and medicine, and most sick people lacked both money for medical care and access to doctors. Now a medical and health network has been established in Tibet, integrated with traditional Chinese, Western and Tibetan medicines, covering all the cities and villages in the region, with Lhasa as the center. Tibetan medicine and pharmacology, with unique ethnic features, are promoted all over China and abroad. By 2000, the medical and health organizations in the region had increased to 1,237, with 6,348 beds and 8,948 professionals. The numbers of hospital beds and health workers available per thousand people in Tibet exceeded the national average level. At present, the cooperative medical service program covers 80 percent of the Tibetan rural areas, and 97 percent of children have been immunized against epidemic diseases. There is no longer any lack of medicine, and the level of the Tibetan people's health has improved substantially. The incidence of various infectious and endemic diseases prevalent in old Tibet, such as smallpox, cholera, venereal diseases, macula, typhoid fever, scarlet fever and tetanus, has declined to eight per thousand, and some of the diseases have been wiped out. The childbirth mortality rate has dropped from 50 per thousand in 1959 to approximately seven per thousand; and the infant mortality rate, from 430 to 6.61 per thousand. The average life expectancy of the people has increased from 35.5 years in the 1950s to the present 67 years. The population of old Tibet had increased rather slowly; over the 200-odd years before the 1950s, it had fluctuated at around one million. (According to the census of the Qing Dynasty government from 1734 to 1736, Tibet had a population of 941,200, and the population reported by the Tibetan local government headed by the Dalai Lama in 1953 was one million, an increase of only 58,000 in 200 years.) However, over the 40-odd years since the Democratic Reform, Tibet's population had increased to 2.5983 million by 2000, or an increase of more than 160 percent.

Considerable achievements have been made in sports. A number of sports facilities up to the international standards have been built in Tibet, and traditional Tibetan sports have been revived, standardized and popularized, some of them even having been included in national competitions. Some excellent athletes from Tibet have scored outstanding achievements in various national sports games and competitions, and in mountain climbing in particular Tibetans have always taken the lead in the country. In 1999, the Sixth National Ethnic Games were held jointly by Tibet and Beijing, further improving the level of Tibetan sports.

> THE FINE ASPECTS OF TRADITIONAL TIBETAN CULTURE HAVE BEEN EXPLORED, PROTECTED AND DEVELOPED.

The state has invested a huge amount of capital, gold and silver in the maintenance and protection of the key historical monuments in Tibet. The Potala Palace and Jokhang Temple have been included in UNESCO's World Cultural Heritage List. The collation of the Tibetan-language Tripitaka (Gangyur and Tengyur) has been completed. Known as an "encyclopedia" of ancient Tibet, the Bonist Tripitaka has been sorted out in a systematic way and published in its entirety. The Life of King Gesar, which had been handed down orally for centuries, has reached the grand total of more than 200 volumes. Thanks to the great support of the state and unremitting efforts in the past few decades, more than 300 handwritten and block-printed copies of this "Homeric epic of the East" have been collected, of which more than 70 volumes have been published in the Tibetan language, over 20 volumes in the Chinese language, and several volumes in English, Japanese and French. Folk songs, dances, dramas, tales and other forms of artistic expression have been refined and imbued with new ideas and higher forms of expression for enjoyment by the general public. The state has invested in the construction of a large number of cultural and recreational facilities with complete functions and advanced facilities in Tibet, such as museums, libraries, exhibition halls and cinemas, in sharp contrast to the old days when Tibet almost had no cultural and recreational facilities to speak of. By 2000, the Tibet Autonomous Region had more than 400 public cultural centers, more than 25 professional theatrical troupes of various kinds, such as the Song and Dance Ensemble, Tibetan Opera Troupe and Modern Drama Troupe of the Tibet Autonomous Region, more than 160 amateur performance troupes, and 17 itinerant performance troupes at the county level. They can meet the demands of the broad masses of the people for cultural entertainment.

➤ TIBETAN'S CHARACTERISTICS AND TRADITIONS HAVE BEEN RESPECTED AND CARRIED ON IN A SCIENTIFIC WAY.

The Tibet Autonomous Region has the right to decide its local affairs and work out relevant laws and regulations in accordance with the law and local political, economic and cultural characteristics, as well as the right to flexibly implement or cease to implement relevant decisions of the state organs at the higher levels, upon approval by the higher authorities. Since 1965, the Regional People's Congress and its Standing Committee have formulated and promulgated more than 160 local laws and regulations, involving the building of political power, economic development, culture and education, spoken and written language, protection of cultural relics, protection of wildlife and natural resources and other aspects, thus effectively safeguarding the special rights and interests of the Tibetan people. For instance, the power and administrative organs of the Tibet Autonomous Region have designated the Tibetan New Year, Shoton (Yogurt) Festival and other traditional Tibetan festivals as the region's official holidays, apart from the official national holidays. Out of consideration for the special natural and geographical factors of Tibet, the region has fixed the work week at 35 hours, five hours fewer than the national work hours per week.

The Tibetan people's freedom of religious belief and their traditional customs and habits have been respected and protected. According to statistics, since the 1980s the state has allocated more than 300 million yuan and a large amount of gold, silver and other materials for the maintenance and protection of the monasteries in Tibet. For instance, the state allocated more than 55 million yuan for the repair of the Potala Palace, and the renovation lasted more than five years, being the largest project and involving the largest amount of capital in the maintenance history of the palace in the past few centuries. At present, Tibet has 1,787 monasteries and sites for religious activities, and over 46,000 resident monks and nuns; the region's various important religious festivals and activities are held normally; and every year more than one million Tibetan people go to Lhasa to pay homage. While maintaining the traditional Tibetan ways and styles of costume, diet and housing, the Tibetan people have absorbed many new modern civilized customs in the aspects of clothing, food, housing and transportation, as well as marriage and funerals, thus greatly enriching their lives.

The Tibetan people's freedom to study, use and develop their own spoken and written language is fully protected. The government has established the special Tibetan Language Work Guidance Committee and editing and translation organs so as to promote the study, use and development of the Tibetan language. The Tibetan language is a major course of study for schools at all levels in Tibet. Tibetan textbooks and reference materials have been compiled, translated and published for all courses at all levels of schools from primary to senior high. Tibet University has compiled 19 varieties of teaching materials in the Tibetan language, which have already been used on a trial basis. The laws and regulations, resolutions, announcements and other official documents issued by the Regional People's Congress and the Regional People's Government, and the name plates and signs of public institutions and sites are written in both the Tibetan and Chinese languages. The courts and procuratorates at all levels handle cases and issue legal documents in the Tibetan language with regard to the Tibetan litigants and other participants. Newspapers, and radio and TV stations use both the Tibetan and Chinese languages. The Tibet People's Radio Station broadcasts Tibetan-language items 20.5 hours a day, making up 50 percent of the station's total broadcasting hours and amount. The Tibet TV Station releases 12 hours of programs in the Tibetan language every day, and the channels in the Tibetan language were formally relayed via satellite in 1999. Now Tibet has 23 Tibetan-language newspapers and magazines, and the Tibet Daily has installed computer editing and typesetting in the Tibetan language. Great progress has been made in the standardization of information technology in the Tibetan language.

The Tibetan code has been brought up to the national and international standards, becoming the first minority written language in China to reach the international standards.

THE PEOPLE'S QUALITY OF LIFE HAS GREATLY IMPROVED.

Social and economic development has improved the people's material and cultural life remarkably. In 2000, people of all ethnic groups in Tibet had basically shaken off poverty, and had enough to eat and wear; and some people were living a fairly comfortable life. Along with the improvement of the people's livelihood, diversified consumption patterns have appeared, and such consumer goods as refrigerators, color TV sets, washing machines, motorcycles and wristwatches have entered ordinary families. Many farmers and herdsmen have become well-off and have built new houses; some have even bought automobiles. Currently, Tibet ranks first in per capita housing in the country. Radio, television, telecommunications, the Internet and other modern information transmission means, which are at the same levels of the country and the rest of the world, are now parts of the Tibetans' daily life. By 2000, the coverage of radio stations had reached 77.7 percent of the population in Tibet, and that of TV stations, 76.1 percent. News about the rest of the country and other parts of the world reach most people in Tibet by means of radio and TV, and they can obtain information from and make contact with other parts of the country and the rest of the world through telephone, telegram, fax or the Internet at any time.

The people's political status has been constantly raised, and their participation in political affairs is becoming more extensive with each passing day. Like the people of other ethnic groups in China, the Tibetan people have the right to vote and stand for election, and extensively participate in the administration of state and local affairs according to law. Of the deputies to the National People's Congress, 19 are from Tibet, of whom over 80 percent are of the Tibetan ethnic group or other ethnic minorities. Of the deputies to the people's congresses at the regional, county and township levels, those from the Tibetan ethnic group and other ethnic minorities make up 82.4 percent, 92. 62 percent and 99 percent, respectively. The main leading posts of the people's congresses, governments, political consultative conferences, and courts and procuratorates at all levels in the region are filled by Tibetan citizens, and Tibetan cadres also hold leading posts in all the state organs at the central level. Of the chairman and vice-chairmen of the Standing Committee of the People's Congress of the Tibet Autonomous Region, Tibetans and people of other ethnic minorities make up 71.4 percent; of the members of the Standing Committee of the Regional People's Congress, 80 percent; and of the chairman and vice-chairmen of the Regional People's Government, 77.8 percent; of the total cadres in Tibet, 79.4 percent; and of all the technical personnel in Tibet, 69.36 percent.

Tibet is still an underdeveloped area in China, because it is located on the "roof of the world," which is frigid, lacks oxygen and has bad natural conditions. Another reason is that Tibet had very little to start with and its social and historical conditions were burdened with the legacy of centuries of backward feudal serfdom. Tibet's economy is small; its development level is low; agriculture, animal husbandry and the ecological environment are fragile; the infrastructure facilities are weak; and science and technology and education are backward. In addition, Tibet lacks the ability for self-accumulation and development, and its modernization level lags far behind that of the southeastern coastal areas of China. But it is beyond doubt that the development of Tibet in the past half century has greatly changed its former poor and backward features, and laid a solid foundation for realizing a leapfrog development in its modernization drive.

I. THE HISTORICAL INEVITABILITY OF TIBET'S MODERNIZATION

Fifty years is a short period in the long process of human history. However, in the past 50 years Tibet, an ancient and mysterious land, has undergone tremendous changes far beyond comparison with those in any other era. Tibet has bidden farewell to the poor, backward, isolated and stagnant feudal serf society, and is forging ahead toward a modern people's democratic society featuring constant progress, civilization and opening-up, and its modernization drive has won world-renowned achievements. First, the situation in which a small number of feudal serf-owners monopolized Tibet's political power and material and cultural resources has been thoroughly changed, and all the people in Tibet have become masters administering Tibetan society, and the creators and beneficiaries of the society's material and cultural wealth. As a result, the people's status and quality have greatly improved. Second, the isolated, stagnant and declining old Tibetan society has been thoroughly smashed; economic development has advanced by leaps and bounds; people's material and cultural life has greatly improved; the modernization drive has developed in an unprecedented way; and an overall-progress situation has appeared in the constant reform and opening-up. Third, Tibet has thoroughly abolished ethnic oppression and discrimination and cleaned up the filth and mire left over from the old Tibetan society; Tibet's ethnic characteristics and the fine aspects of its traditional culture have won full respect and protection under the regional ethnic autonomy system; with the progress of the modernization drive, they have been imbued with the current contents that reflect the people's new life and the new requirements of social progress, and have thus been carried forward in a process of scientific inheritance.

The development in the past 50 years has demonstrated the historical inevitability of Tibet's march toward modernization, and revealed the objective law of Tibet's modernization.

> TIBET'S MARCH TOWARD MODERNIZATION CONFORMS TO THE WORLD HISTORICAL TREND AND THE LAW OF DEVELOPMENT OF HUMAN SOCIETY, AND EMBODIES THE INTERNAL DEMANDS OF TIBET'S SOCIAL DEVELOPMENT AND THE FUNDAMENTAL INTERESTS AND WISHES OF THE TIBETAN PEOPLE.

Realizing modernization has been a common issue facing all countries and regions in the world in modern times, as well as a natural historical course when human society is changing from an underdeveloped state to a developed one, from ignorance and backwardness to civilization and progress, from relatively independent development in a closed society to high-speed development in an all-round way in opening-up, cooperation and competition. At the very beginning, modernization appeared following the rise and expansion of the capitalist countries in the West. For a considerable length of time, the big powers in the West monopolized the fruits of modernization and used them in the invasion and colonial rule in the Third World countries. With the rise of the decolonization movement in the 20th century, getting rid of poverty and backwardness and realizing modernization became the road that the Third World countries had to take to realize their complete independence and the invigoration of their nations. Historical development has proved that the modernization tide is enormous and powerful, that those who go with it will prosper while those who go against it will perish. Tibet's productive forces, mode of production and social and political systems in the modern era were in the extremely backward state of the Middle Ages, and came near the verge of collapse after Tibet was subject to imperialist invasion and control. Ending imperialist invasion and control, reforming the backward social and political systems and mode of production and realizing modernization have historically become the only way out and the most urgent question for social progress in Tibet. Since the founding of the

People's Republic of China in 1949, Tibet, through the peaceful liberation, Democratic Reform, socialist construction, and reform and opening-up, has broken away from the clutches of imperialism, entered the modern society of people's democracy from the feudal serf society that lagged far behind the times, realized high-speed economic development and all- round social development, and headed toward modernization step by step. All these comply with the world tide of modernization and the law of development of human society, and embody the demand for social progress in Tibet and the fundamental aspiration of the Tibetan people.

> ➢ TIBET'S MODERNIZATION IS AN INSEPARABLE PART OF CHINA'S MODERNIZATION DRIVE, AND THE INEVITABLE DEMAND FROM THE PEOPLE OF ALL ETHNIC GROUPS IN CHINA TO REALIZE COMMON PROSPERITY AND THE CHINESE NATION TO REALIZE GREAT REJUVENATION.

In the centuries-long course of historical development, our 56 ethnic groups, including the Tibetan ethnic group, have jointly developed China's territory, and formed the big family of the Chinese nation, in which all the ethnic groups share weal and woe, and are inseparable from each other. As an integral part of Chinese territory, Tibet has always gone through thick and thin together with the motherland for common development. Tibet's progress and development are closely related to those of the motherland, and the motherland's destiny directly affects Tibet's future. In modern times, China was reduced to a semi-colonial and semi-feudal society; Chinese territory, including Tibet, was subject to invasion and devastation by the big powers of the West; and China was confronted with the fate of being carved up and dismembered because of its weak national strength and the corruption and incompetence of feudal autocracy. Along with the victory of the national democratic revolution in China and the founding of the

People's Republic of China, Tibet realized peaceful liberation, drove away the imperialist forces, took the course of modernization, threw off the heavy shackles of feudal serfdom through the Democratic Reform, and smoothed the road to modernization. As Tibet is a relatively backward area, its development has always been the concern of the Central Government and the people of all ethnic groups in China. In the past 50 years, the state has paid special attention to the social and economic development of Tibet. It has given a powerful impetus to Tibet's modernization by granting it special preferential policies in terms of finance, tax revenue, banking and other aspects, offering energetic support in capital, technology and human resources, investing an accumulative total of close to 50 billion yuan, sending a large amount of materials and dispatching a large number of cadres and technical personnel to help Tibet. We may well say that Tibet's progress and development in the past 50 years has been achieved under the correct leadership of the three generations of leading collectives of the central authorities, with Mao Zedong, Deng Xiaoping and Jiang Zemin at the core in different periods. This has been inseparable from the unification and development of the motherland and the selfless support of the whole nation; it is also a vivid embodiment of the new ethnic relations of equality, unity, mutual help and common development among all ethnic groups in China.

History has proved that Tibet's modernization cannot be separated from that of the motherland, and the motherland's modernization cannot be realized without that of Tibet. Without Tibet's modernization, the motherland's modernization would be incomplete and incomprehensive. Without the independence and prosperity of the motherland, Tibetan society would not have new life and development. Only when Tibet's modernization drive is merged with the motherland's modernization and wins the support and help of the people throughout the country, can Tibet tightly grasp the historical opportunities, realize speedy development, and achieve constant progress and prosperity. The vigorous development of the motherland's modernization is powerful backing for Tibet's modernization. The correct leadership and sturdy support of the Central Government and the selfless support of the people of all ethnic groups in China are the powerful guarantee and necessary conditions for the speedy and healthy development of Tibet's modernization drive.

> ➤ THE MODERNIZATION DRIVE OF TIBET IS THE COMMON CAUSE OF THE PEOPLE OF ALL THE ETHNIC GROUPS THERE. THE FOCUS MUST BE PUT ON MAN, SO AS TO PROMOTE THE ALL-ROUND SOCIAL PROGRESS AND SUSTAINABLE DEVELOPMENT.

The course of Tibet's development over the past 50 years has been a process of continuous human emancipation and advance, as well as the all-round progress of society and the harmonious development of modernization and the environment. The people of all ethnic groups in Tibet have always been the mainstay and basic motive power behind the region's modernization drive, and also the beneficiaries of the results of its development. Tibet's peaceful liberation and the Democratic Reform emancipated the people of all ethnic groups in Tibet from imperialist invasion and the inhuman bonds of the feudal serfdom, making them masters of the nation and the Tibetan society. They showed enormous enthusiasm and exerted all their strength, and became the principal force propelling Tibet's modernization. With the sense of responsibility as the masters of their society, they took an active part in the great cause of building a new Tibet and a new life. They struggled in concert, advanced with a pioneering spirit, laid the first stone for the construction with arduous efforts, and upheld the principle that economic construction and social progress should be undertaken simultaneously, and the economy and environment developed harmoniously. In this way, they gave a mighty thrust to the modernization process of Tibet. The achievements attained in the 50 years of Tibet's modernization drive have fully demonstrated the success of the struggle of the people of all ethnic groups in Tibet and embodied the enormous strength of the Tibetan people. Experience has shown that the concerted struggle of the people of all ethnic groups in Tibet is the dynamo propelling the region's modernization drive. Only by maximizing the zeal, initiative and creativity of the people in Tibet and channeling the concern of the Central Government and the support of other parts of the country into Tibet's own advantages for development can miracles be created in Tibet's modernization drive. Moreover, only by proceeding from the fundamental interests and needs of the Tibetan people and adhering to the sustainable development strategy can Tibet's modernization drive develop quickly and soundly.

> AS TIBET'S MODERNIZATION DRIVE IS UNFOLDING IN THE UNIQUE AREA OF TIBET, IT MUST PROCEED FROM TIBET'S ACTUAL CONDITIONS AND TAKE THE ROAD WITH TIBET'S LOCAL CHARACTERISTICS.

Located on the Qinghai-Tibet Plateau, Tibet is completely different from other regions in geographic environment, natural conditions, historical development, ethnic composition, religious beliefs, cultural traditions, lifestyle and customs. The region's modernization drive must proceed from the actual conditions of Tibet and take into account Tibet's history and reality. Its primary aim should be to spur the development of Tibet's productive forces and social progress, as well as the development and welfare of the people of Tibet. The adverse natural conditions, backward social and economic basis and the complicated background of Tibet's historical development in modern times dictate that Tibet must take modernization as the key link and realize rapid development with special support and help from the Central Government and the rest of the country. In addition, to realize the sustainable, all-round and harmonious development of society and the economy, Tibet must correctly handle the relations between reform, development and stability, utilize natural resources rationally and protect the ecological environment.

For historical reasons, most of the Tibetans in the region are religious believers and religious influences have permeated Tibetan culture, art, social customs and daily life. How to correctly handle the ethnic and religious problems is a long-standing issue of great importance in Tibet's modernization drive. The 50-year development of Tibet shows that accelerating modernization is where the basic interests of the people in Tibet lie, and also the key to the realization of ethnic equality and common development. It is an important guarantee for the sound development of Tibet's modernization drive to uphold the system of regional ethnic autonomy, ensure in practice that the people of all ethnic groups in Tibet, especially the Tibetan people, exercise the right of self-government in administering local affairs according to law, and completely respect their culture and traditions, customs and habits, spoken and written language, and religious beliefs. Only by observing the following principles can a modernization road with Tibetan local and ethnic characteristics be opened up: Focusing on economic construction; upholding the policies of reform and opening-up; combining the protection of the freedom of religious belief with separation of religion from politics; actively guiding religion to gear to the needs of modernization and social progress; and maintaining and promoting Tibet's ethnic characteristics while energetically developing modern industries, science, education and culture, and propelling the modernization of Tibet's traditional industries and culture.

> THE MODERNIZATION DRIVE OF TIBET HAS BEEN FORGING AHEAD CONSISTENTLY DURING THE PROTRACTED STRUGGLE AGAINST THE DALAI LAMA CLIQUE AND INTERNATIONAL HOSTILE FORCES.

As the question of Tibet's modernization emerged against a complicated historical background, it was inevitable that the modernization in

Tibet was connected with international struggles. Over a long period of time, between the Dalai Lama clique and international hostile forces on the one hand and the Chinese Government and people on the other, there have been struggles on the "Tibet issue," with the former trying to split Tibet from the rest of China and halt its modernization, and the latter trying to maintain the unity of the country and promote Tibet's modernization. In modern times, a handful of the political and religious rulers in Tibet, in order to safeguard the vested interests of the serf-owner class and the crumbling feudal serfdom, tried by hook or by crook to hinder the modernization of Tibetan society, and even went so far as to collaborate with the imperialist aggressor forces to unleash the "Tibet independence" campaign, in an attempt to split the country and prevent the peaceful liberation of Tibet. After Tibet's peaceful liberation, the Dalai Lama clique, regardless of the patient forbearance of the Central Government and the strong demand of the Tibetan people, spared no efforts to try to check the Democratic Reform and modernization drive, and, with the support of international hostile forces, stirred up an armed rebellion for the purpose of splitting the motherland. When the rebellion had failed and the Dalai Lama clique fled abroad, it even did not scruple to collude with the international anti-China forces to constantly whip up world opinion, wantonly conduct activities aimed at splitting China, slander Tibet's achievements in economic construction and social progress, and by every means hinder and sabotage the modernization of Tibetan society.

The Dalai Lama clique and international hostile forces slandered the peaceful liberation of Tibet and the expulsion of the imperialist forces from Tibet as "China's occupation of Tibet"; denigrated the Central Government's efforts to propel Tibet's modernization as the "elimination of Tibet's ethnic characteristics"; misrepresented the rapid growth of Tibet's economy as "destruction of Tibet's environment"; vilified the concern and support of the Central Government and the whole nation for the modernization of Tibet as "plundering Tibet's resources," "intensifying control over Tibet" and "Han-Chinese assimilation of Tibet"; calumniated the abolition of theocracy and the secular privileges of the clergy and monasteries as "extinguishing religion"; distorted the promotion of traditional Tibetan culture in the new era and the unprecedented development of modern science, education and culture in Tibet as "extirpation of Tibetan culture, " and so on and so forth. In a word, whatever was beneficial to Tibet's modernization and social progress and the happiness of the Tibetan people, they willfully misrepresented and left no stone unturned to oppose. This fully reveals the reactionary nature of the Dalai Lama clique, which represents the backward relations of production of feudal serfdom, the retrogressive religious culture of the theocratic system, and the interests of the dying privileged few of the feudal serf-owner class. Besides, it fully exposes the sinister mentality of some hostile foreign forces in their vain attempt to utilize the "Tibet issue" to sabotage the stability of China, split China's territory, and prevent China from developing and prospering.

Facts speak louder than words, and people have a sense of natural justice. It is universally acknowledged that Tibet is a part of China's territory, and the progress made by the Tibetan community is there for all to see. China has conformed to the trend of the times and followed the wishes of the people in its efforts to promote the modernization of Tibet and combat the Dalai Lama clique's separatist activities. It is only right and proper to do so. The history of 50 years since the peaceful liberation of Tibet shows that the trend of the times cannot be checked, and the tide of history is irreversible. Tibet's modernization and social progress are part of the general trend and popular feeling. Any lie will certainly be revealed by the objective facts of Tibet's development; any perverse acts to turn the clock back, prevent Tibet's modernization drive and separate Tibet from China are doomed to ignominious failure.

Human society has ushered in a new century, and peace and development are the two major themes in the world today. China has embarked upon the new development stage of building, in a comprehensive way, a society in which people enjoy a fairly comfortable life, and of accelerating the reform and opening-up and modernization + a stage in which the strategy of large-scale development of the western region, as a part of the third-step development strategy of China's modernization drive, is being carried out in an all-round way. With a view to national development and the actual conditions in Tibet, the Fourth Forum on Work in Tibet convened by the Central Government set the strategic objectives for promoting Tibet's modernization in the new century, from simply speeding it up to ensuring a leap forward. The forum also determined to further intensify support for Tibet's development. In this regard, during the Tenth Five-Year Plan period (2001–2005) the Central Government and various parts of the country are to invest 32.2 billion yuan to assist Tibet in constructing 187 projects, and the Central Government is to subsidize Tibet to the tune of 37.9 billion yuan. In addition, other special preferential policies and measures are to be formulated. All this has created new and favorable conditions and rare opportunities for Tibet's modernization drive. It can be confidently asserted that, on the solid foundation laid over the last 50 years and with energetic support and help from the Central Government and people all over the country, Tibet will ultimately realize vigorous development in the process of its modernization drive through arduous efforts, and witness a still more brilliant and splendid future.

NOTES

1. Melvyn C. Goldstein, A History of Modern Tibet (1913–1951) + The Demise of the Lamaist State, University of California Press, Berkeley, Los Angeles, London, 1989–1991, pp. 37 and 2.2. Dongka Lobsang Chilai, On the System of Theocracy in Tibet, Ethnic Minorities Publishing House, 1985. Translated by Chen Qingying, pp. 72-73.3. Ngapoi Ngawang Jigme, A Great Turn in the Development of Tibetan History, published in the first issue of the China Tibetology quarterly, 1991, Beijing.

Appendix IV

Five Point Peace Plan for Tibet
—Address to Members of the United States Congress

by Dalai Lama

Washington, D.C.
September 21, 1987
Source: http://www.tibet.com/Proposal/5point.html

The world is increasingly interdependent, so that lasting peace - national, regional, and global - can only be achieved if we think in terms of broader interest rather than parochial needs. At this time, it is crucial that all of us, the strong and the weak, contribute in our own way. I speak to you today as the leader of the Tibetan people and as a Buddhist monk devoted to the principles of a religion based on love and compassion. Above all, I am here as a human being who is destined to share this planet with you and all others as brothers and sisters. As the world grows smaller, we need each other more than in the past. This is true in all parts of the world, including the continent I come from.

At present in Asia, as elsewhere, tensions are high. There are open conflicts in the Middle East, Southeast Asia, and in my own country,

Tibet. To a large extent, these problems are symptoms of the underlying tensions that exist among the area's great powers. In order to resolve regional conflicts, an approach is required that takes into account the interests of all relevant countries and peoples, large and small. Unless comprehensive solutions are formulated, that take into account the aspirations of the people most directly concerned, piecemeal or merely expedient measures will only create new problems.

The Tibetan people are eager to contribute to regional and world peace, and I believe they are in a unique position to do so. Traditionally, Tibetans are a peace loving and non-violent people. Since Buddhism was introduced to Tibet over one thousand years ago, Tibetans have practiced non-violence with respect to all forms of life. This attitude has also been extended to our country's international relations. Tibet's highly strategic position in the heart of Asia, separating the continent's great powers - India, China and the USSR - has throughout history endowed it with an essential role in the maintenance of peace and stability. This is precisely why, in the past, Asia's empires went to great lengths to keep one another out of Tibet. Tibet's value as an independent buffer state was integral to the region's stability.

When the newly formed People's Republic of China invaded Tibet in 1949/50, it created a new source of conflict. This was highlighted when, following the Tibetan national uprising against the Chinese and my flight to India in 1959, tensions between China and India escalated into the border war in 1962. Today large numbers of troops are again massed on both sides of the Himalayan border and tension is once more dangerously high.

The real issue, of course, is not the Indo-Tibetan border demarcation. It is China's illegal occupation of Tibet, which has given it direct access to the Indian sub-continent. The Chinese authorities have attempted to confuse the issue by claiming that Tibet has always been a part of China. This is untrue. Tibet was a fully independent state when the People's Liberation Army invaded the country in 1949/50.

Since Tibetans emperors unified Tibet, over a thousand years ago, our country was able to maintain its independence until the middle of this century. At times Tibet extended its influence over neighboring countries and peoples and, in other periods, came itself under the influence of powerful foreign rulers - the Mongol Khans, the Gorkhas of Nepal, the Manchu Emperors and the British in India.

It is, of course, not uncommon for states to be subjected to foreign influence or interference,. Although so-called satellite relationships are perhaps the clearest examples of this, most major powers exert influence over less powerful allies or neighbors. As the most authoritative legal studies have shown, in Tibet's case, the country's occasional subjection to foreign influence never entailed a loss of independence. And there can be no doubt that when Peking's communist armies entered Tibet, Tibet was in all respects an independent state.

China's aggression, condemned by virtually all nations of the free world, was a flagrant violation of international law. As China's military occupation of Tibet continues, the world should remember that though Tibetans have lost their freedom, under international law Tibet today is still an independent state under illegal occupation.

It is not my purpose to enter a political/legal discussion here concerning Tibet's status. I just wish to emphasize the obvious and undisputed fact that we Tibetans are a distinct people with our own culture, language, religion and history. But for China's occupation, Tibet would still, today, fulfill its natural role as a buffer state maintaining and promoting peace in Asia.

It is my sincere desire, as well as that of the Tibetan people, to restore to Tibet her invaluable role, by converting the entire country - comprising the three provinces of U-Tsang, Kham and Amdo - once more into a place of stability, peace and harmony. In the best of Buddhist tradition, Tibet would extend its services and hospitality to all who further the cause of world peace and the well-being of mankind and the natural environment we share.

Despite the holocaust inflicted upon our people in the past decades of occupation, I have always strived to find a solution through direct and honest discussions with the Chinese. In 1982, following the change of leadership in China and the establishment of direct contacts with the government in Peking, I sent my representatives to Peking to open talks concerning the future of my country and people.

We entered the dialogue with a sincere and positive attitude and with a willingness to take into account the legitimate needs of the People's Republic of China. I hope that this attitude would be reciprocated and that a solution could eventually be found which would satisfy and safeguard the aspirations and interests of both parties. Unfortunately, China has consistently responded to our efforts in a defensive manner, as though our detailing of Tibet's very real difficulties was criticism for its own sake.

To our even greater dismay, the Chinese government misused the opportunity for a genuine dialogue. Instead of addressing the real issues facing the six million Tibetan people, China has attempted to reduce the question of Tibet to a discussion of my own personal status.

It is against this background and in response to the tremendous support and encouragement I have been given by you and other persons I have met during this trip, that I wish today to clarify the principal issues and to propose, in a spirit of openness and conciliation, a first step towards a lasting solution. I hope this may contribute to a future of friendship and cooperation with all of our neighbors, including the Chinese people.

This peace plan contains five basic components:

1. Transformation of the whole of Tibet into a zone of peace;
2. Abandonment of China's population transfer policy which threatens the very existence of the Tibetan's as a people;
3. Respect for the Tibetan people's fundamental human rights and democratic freedoms;
4. Restoration and protection of Tibet's natural environment and the abandonment of China's use of Tibet for the production of nuclear weapons and dumping of nuclear waste;
5. Commencement of earnest negotiations on the future status of Tibet and of relations between the Tibetan and Chinese peoples.

Let me explain these five components.

➢ 1

I propose that the whole of Tibet, including the eastern provinces of Kham and Amdo, be transformed into a zone of "Ahimsa", a Hindi term used to mean a state of peace and non-violence. The establishment of such a peace zone would be in keeping with Tibet's historical role as a peaceful and neutral Buddhist nation and buffer state separating the continent's great powers. It would also be in keeping with Nepal's proposal to proclaim Nepal a peace zone and with China's declared support for such a proclamation. The peace zone proposed by Nepal would have a much greater impact if it were to include Tibet and neighboring areas.

The establishing of a peace zone in Tibet would require withdrawal of Chinese troops and military installations from the country, which would enable India also to withdraw troops and military installations from the Himalayan regions bordering Tibet. This would be achieved under an international agreement which would satisfy China's legitimate security needs and build trust among the Tibetan, Indian, Chinese and other peoples of the region. This is in everyone's best interest, particularly that of China and India, as it would enhance their security, while reducing the economic burden of maintaining high troop concentrations on the disputed Himalayan border.

Historically, relations between China and India were never strained. It was only when Chinese armies marched into Tibet, creating for the first time a common border, that tensions arose between these two powers, ultimately leading to the 1962 war. Since then numerous dangerous incidents have continued to occur. A restoration of good relations between the world's two most populous countries would be greatly facilitated if they were separated - as they were throughout history - by a large and friendly buffer region.

To improve relations between the Tibetan people and the Chinese, the first requirement is the creation of trust. After the holocaust of the last decades in which over one million Tibetans - one sixth of the population - lost their lives and at least as many lingered in prison camps because of their religious beliefs and love of freedom, only a withdrawal of Chinese troops could start a genuine process of reconciliation. The vast occupation force in Tibet is a daily reminder to the Tibetans of the oppression and suffering they have all experienced. A troop withdrawal would be an essential signal that in the future a meaningful relationship might be established with the Chinese, based on friendship and trust.

➢ 2

The population transfer of Chinese into Tibet, which the government in Peking pursues in order to force a "final solution" to the Tibetan problem by reducing the Tibetan population to an insignificant and disenfranchised minority in Tibet itself, must be stopped.

The massive transfer of Chinese civilians into Tibet in violation of the Fourth Geneva Convention (1949) threatens the very existence of the Tibetans as a distinct people. In the eastern parts of our country, the Chinese now greatly outnumber Tibetans. In the Amdo province, for example, where I was born, there are, according to Chinese statistics, 2.5 million Chinese and only 750,000 Tibetans. Even in so-called Tibet Autonomous Region (i.e., central and western Tibet), Chinese government sources now confirm that Chinese outnumber Tibetans.

The Chinese population transfer policy is not new. It has been systematically applied to other areas before. Earlier in this century, the Manchus were a distinct race with their own culture and traditions. Today only two to three million Manchurians are left in Manchuria, where 75 million Chinese have settled. In Eastern Turkestan, which the Chinese now call Sinkiang, the Chinese population has grown from 200,000 in 1949 to 7 million, more than half of the total population of 13 million. In the wake of the Chinese colonization of Inner Mongolia, Chinese number 8.5 million, Mongols 2.5 million.

Today, in the whole of Tibet 7.5 million Chinese settlers have already been sent, outnumbering the Tibetan population of 6 million. In central and western Tibet, now referred to by the Chinese as the "Tibet Autonomous Region", Chinese sources admit the 1.9 million Tibetans already constitute a minority of the region's population. These numbers do not take the estimated 300,000 - 500,000 troops in Tibet into account - 250,000 of them in the so-called Tibet Autonomous Region. For the Tibetans to survive as a people, it is imperative that the population transfer is stopped and Chinese settlers return to China. Otherwise, Tibetans will soon be no more than a tourist attraction and relic of a noble past.

➤ 3

Fundamental human rights and democratic freedoms must be respected in Tibet. The Tibetan people must once again be free to develop culturally, intellectually, economically and spiritually and to exercise basic democratic freedoms.

Human rights violations in Tibet are among the most serious in the world. Discrimination is practiced in Tibet under a policy of "apartheid" which the Chinese call "segregation and assimilation". Tibetans are, at best, second class citizens in their own country. Deprived of all basic democratic rights and freedoms, they exist under a colonial administration in which all real power is wielded by Chinese officials of the Communist Party and the army.

Although the Chinese government allows Tibetan to rebuild some Buddhist monasteries and to worship in them, it still forbids serious study and teaching of religion. Only a small number of people, approved by the Communist Party, are permitted to join the monasteries.

While Tibetans in exile exercise their democratic rights under a constitution promulgated by me in 1963, thousands of our countrymen suffer in prisons and labor camps in Tibet for their religious or political convictions.

➤ 4

Serious efforts must be made to restore the natural environment in Tibet. Tibet should not be used for the production of nuclear weapons and the dumping of nuclear waste.

Tibetans have a great respect for all forms of life. This inherent feeling is enhanced by the Buddhist faith, which prohibits the harming of all sentient beings, whether human or animal. Prior to the Chinese invasion, Tibet was an unspoiled wilderness sanctuary in a unique natural environment. Sadly, in the past decades the wildlife and the forests of Tibet have been almost totally destroyed by the Chinese. The effects on Tibet's delicate environment have been devastating. What little is left in Tibet must be protected and efforts must be made to restore the environment to its balanced state.

China uses Tibet for the production of nuclear weapons and may also have started dumping nuclear waste in Tibet. Not only does China plan to dispose of its own nuclear waste but also that of other countries, who have already agreed to pay Peking to dispose of their toxic materials. The dangers this presents are obvious. Not only living generations, but future generations are threatened by China's lack of concern for Tibet's unique and delicate environment.

➤ 5

Negotiations on the future status of Tibet and the relationship between the Tibetan and Chinese peoples should be started in earnest. We wish to approach this subject in a reasonable and realistic way, in a spirit of frankness and conciliation and with a view to finding a solution that in the long term interest of all: the Tibetans, the Chinese, and all other peoples concerned. Tibetans and Chinese are distinct peoples, each with their own country, history, culture, language and way of life. Differences among peoples must be recognized and respected. They need not, however, form obstacles to genuine cooperation where this is in the mutual benefit of both peoples. It is my sincere belief that if the concerned parties were to meet and discuss their future with an open mind and a sincere desire to find a satisfactory and just solution, a breakthrough could be achieved. We must all exert ourselves to be reasonable and wise, and to meet in a spirit of frankness and understanding.

Let me end on a personal note. I wish to thank you for the concern and support which you and so many of your colleagues and fellow citizens have expressed for the plight of oppressed people everywhere. The fact that you have publicly shown your sympathy for us Tibetans, has already had a positive impact on the lives of our people inside Tibet. I ask for your continued support in this critical time in our country's history.

APPENDIX V

Dalai Lama's letters to Deng Xiaoping and Jiang Zemin

September 11, 1992

Source: http://www.tibet.com/Proposal/sino-tibet.html#C4

On June 22, 1992, Mr. Ding Guangen, head of the United Front Works Department of CCP Central Committee, met with Mr. Gyalo Thondup in Beijing and restated the assurance given by Mr. Deng Xiaoping to Mr. Gyalo Thondup in 1979 that the Chinese government was willing to discuss and any issue with us except total independence. Mr. Ding Guangen also said that, in the government's view, "the Dalai Lama is continuing with independence activities," but the Chinese government was willing to immediately start negotiations as soon as I give up the independence of Tibet. This position, repeatedly stated in the past by the Chinese government, shows that the Chinese leadership still does not understand my ideas regarding the Tibetan-Chinese relationship. Therefore, I take this opportunity to clarify my position through this note.

1. It is an established fact that Tibet and China existed as separate countries in the past. However, as a result of misrepresentations of Tibet's unique relations with the Mongol and the Manchu Emperors. disputes arose between Tibet and the Kuomintang and the present

Chinese government. The fact that the Chinese government found it necessary to conclude a "17-Point Agreement" with the Tibetan government in 1951 clearly shows the Chinese government's acknowledgement of Tibet's unique position.

2. When I visited Beijing in 1954, I had the impression that most of the Communist party leaders I met there were honest, straightforward and open minded. Chairman Mao Zedong, in particular, told me on several occasions that the Chinese were in Tibet only to help Tibet harness its natural resources and use them for the development of the country; General Zhang Jingwu and General Fan Ming, were in Tibet to help me and the people of Tibet, and not to rule the Tibetan government and people. and that all Chinese officials in Tibet were there to help us and to be withdrawn when Tibet had progressed. Any Chinese official who did not act accordingly! would be sent back to China. Chairman Mao went on to say that it had now been decided to establish a "Preparatory Committee for the Establishment of the Tibet Autonomous Region" instead of the earlier plan to put Tibet under the direct control of the Chinese government through a "Military-Political Commission."

At my last meeting with Chairman Mao, before I left China. he gave me a long explanation about democracy. He said that I must provide leadership and advised me on how to keep in touch with the views of the people. He spoke in a gentle and compassionate manner which was moving and inspiring.

While in Beijing, I told Premier Zhou Enlai that we Tibetans were fully aware of our need to develop politically, socially and economically and that in fact I had already taken steps towards this.

On my way back to Tibet, I told General Zhang Guohua that I had gone to China with doubts and anxiety about the future of my people and country, but had now returned with great hope and optimism and a very positive impression of the Chinese leaders. My innate desire to serve my people, especially the poor and the weak, and the prospect of mutual cooperation and friendship between Tibet and China made me feel hopeful and optimistic about Tibet's future development. This was how I felt at that time about the Tibetan-Chinese relationship.

3. When the "Tibet Autonomous Region Preparatory Committee" was setup in Lhasa in 1956, there was no alternative but to work sincerely with it for the interest and benefit of both parties. However, by then the Chinese authorities had already started to use unthinkable brutal force to impose Communism on the Tibetan people of the Kham and Amdo areas, particularly in Lithang. This increased the resentment of the Tibetans against Chinese policies, leading to open resistance.

I could not believe that Chairman Mao would have approved of such repressive policy because of the promises he had made to me when I was in China. I, therefore, wrote three letters to him explaining the situation and seeking an end to the repression. Regrettably, there was no reply to my letters.

In late 1956, I visited India to attend Buddha Jayanti, the anniversary of the birth of Buddha. At that time, many Tibetans advised me not to return to Tibet, and to continue talks with China from India. I also felt that I should stay in India for the time being. While in India, I met Premier Zhou Enlai and told him how deeply saddened I was by the military repression inflicted upon Tibetans in Kham and Amdo in the name of "reforms." Premier Zhou Enlai said that he regarded these matters as mistakes committed by Chinese officials and that "reforms" in Tibet would be carried out only in accordance with the wishes of the

Tibetan people, and that in fact the Chinese government had already decided to postpone the "reforms" in Tibet by six years. He then urged me to return to Tibet as soon as possible in order to prevent further outbreaks of unrest.

According to the Indian Prime Minister, Jawaharlal Nehru, Premier Zhou Enlai told him that the Chinese government "did not consider Tibet as a province of China. The people were different from the people of China proper. Therefore, they (the Chinese) considered Tibet as an autonomous region which could enjoy autonomy." Prime Minister Nehru told me that he had assurances from Premier Zhou Enlai that Tibet's autonomy would be respected and, therefore, advised me to make efforts to safeguard it and cooperate with China in bringing about reforms.

By then, the situation in Tibet had become extremely dangerous and desperate. Nevertheless, I decided to return to Tibet to give the Chinese government another opportunity to be able to implement their promises. On my return to Lhasa through Dromo, Gyangtse and Shigatse I had many meetings with Tibetan and Chinese officials; I told them that the Chinese were not in Tibet to rule the Tibetans, that the Tibetans were not subjects of China, and that since the Chinese leaders had promised to establish Tibet as an autonomous region with full internal freedoms, we all had to work to make it succeed. I emphasised the point that the leaders of China had assured me that all Chinese personnel in Tibet were there to help us, and that if they behaved otherwise, they would be going against the order of their own government. I believe, I was once again doing my best to promote cooperation between Tibet and China.

4. However, because of the harsh military repression in the Kham and Amdo parts of eastern Tibet, thousands of young and old Tibetans

unable to live under such circumstances, began to arrive in Lhasa as refugees. As a result of these Chinese actions the Tibetan people felt great anxiety and began to lose faith in the promises made by China. This led to greater resentment and a worsening of the situation. Nevertheless, I continued to counsel my people to seek a peaceful solution and to show restraint. At the risk of losing the trust of the Tibetan people 1 did my best to prevent a break-down of the communications with the Chinese officials in Lhasa . But the situation continued to deteriorate and finally exploded in the tragic events of 1959 which forced me to leave Tibet. Faced with such a desperate situation. I had no alternative but to appeal lo the United Nations. The United Nations, in turn passed three resolutions on Tibet in 1959, 1961 and 1965, wherein it called for the cessation of practices which deprived Tibetan people of their fundamental human rights and freedoms including their right to self- determination" and asked member States to make all possible efforts toward achieving that purpose.

The Chinese government did not respect the United Nations resolutions. In the meantime, the Cultural Revolution started and there was absolutely no opportunity for solving the Tibetan-Chinese problems. It was, in fact, not even possible to identify a leader with whom we could talk.

5. Despite of my unfulfilled hopes and disappointments in dealing with the Chinese government, and since Tibet and China, will always remain as neighbors. I am convinced that we must strive to find a way to co-exist in peace and help each other. This, I believe, is possible and worthy of our efforts. With this conviction I said in my statement to the Tibetan people on March 10, 1971: "Despite of the fact that we Tibetans have to oppose Communist China, I can never bring myself to hate her people. Hatred is not a sign of strength, but of weakness. When Lord Buddha said that hatred cannot be overcome by hatred, he was not only

being spiritual. But His words reflect the practical reality of life. What ever one achieves through hatred will not last long. On the other hand, hatred will only generate more problems. And for the Tibetan people who are faced with such a tragic situation, hatred will only bring additional depression. Moreover, how can we hate a people who do not know what they are doing? How can we hate millions of Chinese, who have no power and are helplessly led by their leaders? We cannot even hate the Chinese leaders for they have suffered tremendously for their nation and the cause which they believe to be right. I do not believe in hatred, but I do believe, as I have always done, that one day truth and justice will triumph."

In my March 10th statement of 1973, referring to the Chinese claim of Tibetans being made the "masters of the country" after being "liberated from the three big feudal lords" and enjoying "unprecedented progress and happiness," I stated: "The aim of the struggle of the Tibetans outside Tibet is the attainment of the happiness of the Tibetan people. If the Tibetans in Tibet are truly happy under Chinese rule then there is no reason for us here in exile to argue otherwise."

Again. in my 1979 March 10th statement, I welcomed Mr. Deng Xiaoping's statement "to seek truth from facts", to give the Chinese people their long cherished rights, and of the need to acknowledge one's own mistakes and shortcomings. While commending these signs of honesty, progress and openness, I said: "The present Chinese leaders should give up the past dogmatic narrow-mindedness and fear of losing face and recognize the present world situation. They should accept their mistakes, the realities, and the right of all peoples of the human race to equality and happiness. Acceptance of this should not be merely on paper; it should be put into practice. If these are accepted and strictly followed, all problems can be solved with honesty and justice." With this conviction I renewed my efforts to promote reconciliation and friendship between China and Tibet.

6. In 1979, Mr. Deng Xiaoping invited Mr. Gyalo Thondup to Beijing and told him that apart from the question of total independence all other issues could be discussed and all problems can be resolved. Mr. Deng further told Mr. Thondup that we must keep in contact with each other and that we could send fact-finding delegations to Tibet. This naturally gave us great hopes of resolving our problem peacefully and we started sending delegations to Tibet.

On March 13, 1981, I sent a letter to Mr. Deng Xiaoping, in which I said, "The three fact-finding delegations have been able to find out both the positive and negative aspects of the situation in Tibet. If the Tibetan people's identity is preserved and if they are genuinely happy, there is no reason to complain. How ever, in reality over 90% of the Tibetans are suffering both mentally and physically, and are living in deep sorrow. These sad conditions had not been brought about by natural disasters, but by human actions. Therefore, genuine efforts must be made to solve the problem in accordance with the existing realities in a reasonable way.

In order to do this, we must improve the relationship between China and Tibet as well as between Tibetans in and outside Tibet. With truth and equality as our foundation, we must try to develop friendship between Tibetans and Chinese in future through better understanding. Time has come to apply our com mon wisdom in a spirit of tolerance and broad-mindedness to achieve genuine happiness for the Tibetan people with a sense of urgency. On my part, I remain committed to contribute to the welfare of all human beings and in particular the poor and the weak to the best of my ability without making any distinction based on national boundaries.

I hope you will let me know you views on the foregoing points." There was no reply to my letter Instead, on July 28, 1981, General Secretary Hu Yaobang gave Mr. Gyalo Thondup a document, entitled "Five point Policy Towards the Dalai Lama."

This was a surprise and a great disappointment. The reason for our consistent efforts to deal with the Chinese government is to achieve lasting and genuine happiness for six million Tibetans who must live as neighbors of China from generation to generation. However, the Chinese leadership chose tc ignore this and, instead, attempted to reduce the whole issue to that of my personal status and the conditions for my return without any willingness to address the real underlying issues. Nevertheless, I continued to place hope in Mr. Deng Xiaoping's statement "seeking truth from facts" and his policy of liberalization.

Therefore, I sent several delegations to Tibet and China and wherever there was an opportunity we explained our views to promote under standing through discussion and dialogue. As initially suggested by Mr. Deng Xiaoping I agreed to send Tibetan teachers from India to improve the education of Tibetans in Tibet. But for one reason or the other the Chinese government did not accept this.

These contacts resulted in four fact finding delegations to Tibet, two delegations to Beijing, and the start of family visitations between the Tibetans in Tibet and in exile. However, these steps did not lead to any substantial progress in resolving the problems between us owing to the rigidity of the Chinese leaders' positions which, I believe, failed to reflect Mr. Deng Xiaoping's policies.

7. Once again, I did not give up hope. This was reflected in my annual March 10th statements to the Tibetan people in 1981, 1983, 1984 and 1985, wherein I said the following:

"...past history has disappeared in the past. What is more relevant is that in the future there actually must be real peace and happiness through developing friendly and meaningful relations between China and Tibet. For this to be realized, it is important for both sides to work hard to have tolerant understanding and be open-minded." (1981)

"The right to express one's ideas and to make every effort to implement them enables people everywhere to be come creative and progressive. This engenders human society to make rapid progress and experience genuine harmony....The deprivation of freedom to express one's views, either by force or by other means, is absolutely anachronistic and a brutal form of oppression....The people of the world will not only oppose it, but will condemn it. Hence, the six million Tibetan people must have the right to preserve, and enhance their cultural identity and religious freedom, the right to determine their own destiny and manage their own affairs, and find fulfillment of their free self-expression, without interference from any quarters. This is reasonable and just." (1983).

"Irrespective of varying degrees of development- and economic disparities, continents, nations, communities, families, in fact, all individuals are dependent on one another for their existence and well-beings. Every human being wishes for happiness and does not want suffering. By clearly realizing this, we must develop mutual compassion, love, and a fundamental sense of justice. In such an atmosphere there is hope that problems between nations and problems within families can be gradually over come and that people can live in peace and harmony. Instead, if people adopt an attitude of selfishness, domination and jealousy, the world at large, as well as individuals, will never enjoy peace and harmony. Therefore, I believe that human relations based on mutual com passion and love is fundamentally important to human happiness." (1984)

"...in order to achieve genuine happiness in any human society, free dom of thought is extremely important. This freedom of thought can only be achieved from mutual trust, mutual understanding and the absence of fear....In the case of Tibet and China too, unless we can remove the state of mutual fear and mistrust, unless we can develop a genuine sense of friendship and goodwill the problems that we face today will continue to exist.

It is important for both of us to learn about one another....It is now for the Chinese to act according to the enlightened ideals and principles of the modern times; to come forward with an open mind and make a serious attempt to know and understand the Tibetan people's view point and their true feelings and aspirations....It is wrong to react with suspicion or offence to the opinions that are contrary to one's own way of thinking. It is essential that differences of opinion be examined and discussed openly. When differing viewpoints are frankly stated and sensibly discussed on an equal footing, the decisions or agreements reached as a result will be genuine and beneficial to all concerned. But so long as there is a contradiction between thought and action, there can never be genuine and meaningful agreements.

So, at this time, I feel the most important thing for us to keep in close contact, to express our views frankly and to make sincere efforts to understand each other. And, through eventual improvement inhuman relationship, I am confident that our problems can be solved to our mutual satisfaction." (1985)

In these and other ways I expressed my views clearly. But, there was no reciprocity to my conciliatory approaches. 8. Since all the exchanges between Tibetans and Chinese yielded no results, I felt compelled to make public my views on the steps necessary for an agreeable solution to the fundamental issues. On September 21,1987, I announced a Five

Point Peace Plan in the United States of America. In its introduction, I said that in the hope of real reconciliation and a lasting solution to the problem, it was my desire to take the first step with this initiative. This plan, I hoped, would in the future contribute to the friendship and cooperation among all the neighbouring countries including the Chinese people for their good and benefit. The basic elements were

1. Transformation of the whole of Tibet into a zone of ahimsa (peace and non-violence);

2. Abandonment of China's population. transfer policy which threatens the very existence of the Tibetans as a people;

3. Respect for the Tibetan people's fundamental human rights and democratic freedoms;

4. Restoration and protection of Tibet's natural environment and the abandonment of China's use of Tibet for the production of nuclear weapons and dumping of nuclear waste;

5. Commencement of earnest negotiations on the future status of Tibet and relations between the Tibetan and the Chinese peoples.

As a response to this initiative, Mr. Yang Mingfu, met Mr. Gyalo Thondup on October 17, 1987 and delivered a message containing five points criticizing me for my above peace initiative and accusing me of having instigated the demonstrations in Lhasa of September 27, 1987 and of having worked against the interests of Tibetan people.

This response, far from giving a serious thought to my sincere proposal for reconciliation, was disappointing and demeaning.

Despite this, I tried once again to clarify our views in a detailed 14-point response on December 17, 1987.

9. On June 15, 1988, at the European Parliament in Strasbourg, I once again elaborated on the Five-Point Peace Plan. I proposed as a framework for negotiations to secure the basic rights of the Tibetan people, China could remain responsible for Tibet's foreign policy and maintain a restricted number of military installations in Tibet for defense until a regional peace conference is convened and Tibet is transformed into a neutral peace sanctuary. I was criticized by many Tibetans for this proposal. My idea was, to make it possible for China and Tibet to stay together in lasting friendship and to secure the right for Tibetans to govern their own country. I sincerely believe that in the future a demilitarized Tibet as a zone of ahimsa will contribute to harmony and peace not only between Tibetans and Chinese. but to all the neighboring countries and the entire region.

10. On September 23, 1988, the Chinese government issued a statement that China was willing to begin negotiations with us. The announcement stated that the date and venue for the negotiations would be left to the Dalai Lama. We welcomed this announcement from Beijing and responded on October 25, 1988, proposing January 1989 as the time and Geneva, an internationally recognized neutral venue, as our choices. We announced that we had a negotiating team ready and named the members of the team.

The Chinese government responded on November 18, 1988, rejecting Geneva and expressing preference for Beijing or else Hong Kong, as the venue. They further stated that my negotiating team could not include "a foreigner" and consist only of "younger people," and that it should have older people, including Mr. Gyalo Thondup: We explained that the foreigner was only a legal advisor and not an actual member of the negotiating team and that Mr. Gyalo Thondup would also be included as an advisor to the team.

With a flexible and open attitude we accommodated the Chinese government's requests and agreed to send representatives to Hong Kong to hold preliminary meetings with representatives of the Chinese government. Unfortunately, when both sides had finally agreed on Hong Kong as the site for preliminary discussions the Chinese government re issued to communicate any further and failed to live up to their own suggestion.

11. Although I championed this proposal for over two years there was no evidence of consideration or even an acknowledgement from the Chinese government.

Therefore, in my March 10th statement in 1991, I was compelled to state that unless the Chinese government responded in the near future I would consider myself free from any obligation to abide by the proposal I made in France.

Since the reappeared to be no benefit from the many solutions I had advocated concerning Tibet and China, I had to find a new way. Therefore, in a speech at Yale University on October 9, 1991, I said:

"…I am considering the possibility of a visit to Tibet as early as possible. I have in mind two purposes for such a visit."

"First, I want to ascertain the situation in Tibet myself on the spot and communicate directly with my people. By doing so, I also hope to help the Chinese leadership to understand the true feelings of Tibetans. It would be important, therefore, for senior Chinese leaders to accompany me on such a visit, and that outside observers, including the press be present to see and report their findings."

"Second, I wish to advise and persuade my people not to abandon non-violence as the appropriate form of struggle. My ability to talk to my our people can be a key factor in bringing about a peaceful solution. My visit could be a new opportunity to promote understanding and create a basis for a negotiated solution."

Unfortunately this overture was immediately opposed by the Chinese Government. At that time, I was asked on many occasions by the press whether I was renewing the call for Tibetan independence since I had declared that the Strasbourg proposal was no longer valid. To these questions, I stated that I did not want to comment.

12. The Chinese government has, with great doubt and suspicion, described our struggle as a movement to restore the "old society" and that it was not in the interest of the Tibetan people but for the personal status and interest of the Dalai Lama. Since my youth, I was aware of the many faults of the existing system in Tibet and wanted to improve it. At that time I started the process of reform in Tibet. Soon after our flight to India we introduced democracy in our exile community, step by step. I repeatedly urged my people to follow this path. As a result, our exiled community now implements a system in full accordance with universal democratic principles. It is impossible for Tibet to ever revert to the old system of government. Whether my efforts for the Tibetan cause are as charged by the Chinese for my personal position and benefit or not is clear from my repeated statements that in a future Tibet, I will not assume any governmental responsibility or hold any political position. Furthermore, this is reflected clearly in the Charter which governs the Tibetan Administration in Exile and in the "Guidelines for Future Tibet's Polity and the Basic Features of Its Constitution," which I announced on February 26, 1992.

In the conclusion of these guideline relationship with its neighbors on equal terms and for mutual benefits. It shall of hostility and enmity." Similarly, in my statement of March 10th, 1992, I stated, "When a genuinely cordial relationship is established between the Tibetans and the Chinese, it will enable us not only to resolve the disputes between our two nations in this century, but will also enable the Tibetans to make a significant contribution through our rich cultural tradition for mental peace among the millions of young Chinese."

My endeavors to establish a personal relationship with Chinese leaders include my offer, presented through your Embassy in New Delhi in the latter part of 1980, for a meeting with General Secretary Hu Yaobang during one of his visits abroad at any convenient place. Again in December 1991, when Premier Li Peng visited New Delhi, I proposed to meet him there. These overtures were to no avail.

13. An impartial review of the above points will clearly show that my ideas and successive efforts have consistently sought solutions that will allow Tibet and China to live together in peace. In the light of these facts it is difficult to understand the purpose of the Chinese government's position that Mr. Deng Xiaoping's statement on Tibet of 1979 still stands and that as soon as "the Dalai Lama gives up his splittist activities," negotiations could start. This position has been repeated over and over again with no specific responses to my many initiatives.

If China wants Tibet to stay with China, then China must create the necessary conditions for this. The time has come now for the Chinese to show the way for Tibet and China to live together in friendship. A detailed step by step outline regarding Tibet's basic status should be spelt out. If such a clear outline is given, regardless of the possibility of an agreement or not, we Tibetans can then make a decision whether to live with China or not. If we Tibetans obtain our basic rights to our satisfaction then we are not incapable of seeing the possible advantages of living with the Chinese.

I trust in the far sightedness and wisdom of China's leaders and hope that they will take into consideration the current global political changes and the need to resolve the Tibetan problem peacefully, promoting genuine lasting friendship between our two neighboring peoples.

APPENDIX VI

Labor Law of the People's Republic of China

Source:http://www.chinalegal.net/

(Adopted at the Eighth Meeting of the Standing Committee of the Eighth National People's Congress on July 5, 1994, promulgated by Order No.28 of the President of the People's Republic of China and effective as of January 1, 1995)

Contents

Chapter I General Provisions 150
Chapter II Promotion of Employment 152
Chapter III Labor Contracts and Collective Contracts 153
Chapter IV Working Hours, Rest and Vacations 159
Chapter V Wages 161
Chapter VI Occupational Safety and Health 162
Chapter VII Special Protection For Female and Juvenile Workers 164
Chapter VIII Vocational Training 165
Chapter IX Social Insurance and Welfare 166
Chapter X Labor Disputes 168
Chapter XI Supervision and Inspection 170
Chapter XII Legal Responsibility 171
Chapter XIII Supplementary Provisions 175

Chapter I General Provisions

Article 1 This Law is formulated in accordance with the Constitution in order to protect the legitimate rights and interests of laborers, readjust labor relationships, establish and safeguard a labor system suited to the socialist market economy, and promote economic development and social progress.

Article 2 This Law applies to all enterprises and individual economic organizations(hereinafter referred to as employing units) within the boundary of the People's Republic of China and laborers who form a labor relationship therewith

State organs, institutional organizations and societies as well as laborers who form a labor contract relationship therewith shall follow this Law.

Article 3 Laborers shall have the right to be employed on an equal basis, choose occupations, obtain remuneration for their labor, take rest, have holidays and leaves, obtain protection of occupational safety and health, receive training vocational skills, enjoy social insurance and welfare, and submit applications for settlement of labor disputes, and other rights relating to labor as stipulated by law.

Laborers shall fulfill their labor tasks, improve their vocational skills, follow rules on occupational safety and health, and observe labor discipline and professional ethics.

Article 4 The employing units shall establish and perfect rules and regulations in accordance with the law so as to ensure that laborers enjoy the right to work and fulfill labor obligations.

Article 5 The State shall take various measures to promote employment, develop vocational education, lay down labor standards, regulate social incomes, perfect social insurance system, coordinate labor relationship, and gradually raise the living standard of laborers.

Article 6 The State shall advocate the participation of laborers in social voluntary labor and the development of their labor competitions and activities of forwarding rational proposals, encourage and protect the scientific research and technical renovation engaged by laborers, as well as their inventions and creations; and commend and award labor models and advanced workers.

Article 7 Laborers shall have the right to participate in and organize trade unions in accordance with the law.

Trade unions shall represent and safeguard the legitimate rights and interests of laborers, and independently conduct their activities in accordance with the law.

Article 8 Laborers shall, through the assembly of staff and workers or their congress, or other forms in accordance with the provisions of laws, rules and regulations, take part in democratic management or consult with the employing units on an equal footing about protection of the legitimate rights and interests of laborers.

Article 9 The labor administrative department of the State Council shall be in charge of the management of labor of the whole country.

The labor administrative departments of the local people's governments at or above the county level shall be in charge of the management of labor in the administrative areas under their respective jurisdiction.

Chapter II Promotion of Employment

Article 10 The State shall create conditions for employment and increase opportunities for employment by means of the promotion of economic and social development.

The State shall encourage enterprises, institutional organizations, and societies to initiate industries or expand businesses for the increase of employment within the scope of the stipulations of laws, and administrative rules and regulations.

The State shall support laborers to get jobs by organizing themselves on a voluntary basis or by engaging in individual businesses.

Article 11 Local people's governments at various levels shall take measures to develop various kinds of job search agencies and provide employment services.

Article 12 Laborers shall not be discriminated against in employment, regardless of their ethnic community, race, sex, or religious belief.

Article 13 Females shall enjoy equal rights as males in employment. It shall not be allowed, in the recruitment of staff and workers, to use sex as a pretext for excluding females form employment or to raise recruitment standards for the females, except for the types of work or posts that are not suitable for females as stipulated by the State.

Article 14 Where there are special stipulations in laws, rules and regulations on the employment of the disabled, the personnel of national minorities, and demobilized army men, such special stipulations shall apply.

Article 15 No employing units shall be allowed to recruit juveniles under the age of 16.

Units of literature and art, physical culture and sport, and special arts and crafts that need to recruit juveniles under the age of 16 must go through the formalities of examination and approval according to the relevant provisions of the State and guarantee their right to compulsory education.

Chapter III Labor Contracts and Collective Contracts

Article 16 A labor contract is the agreement reached between a laborer and an employing unit for the establishment of the labor relationship and the definition of the rights, interests and obligations of each party.

A labor contract shall be concluded where a labor relationship is to be established.

Article 17 Conclusion and modification of a labor contract shall follow the principles of equality, voluntaries and unanimity through consultation, and shall not run counter to the stipulations of laws, administrative rules and regulations.

A labor contract once concluded in accordance with the law shall possess legal binding force. The parties involved must fulfill the obligations as stipulated in the labor contract.

Article 18 The following labor contracts shall be invalid:

labor contracts concluded in violation of laws, administrative rules and regulations; and

labor contracts concluded by resorting to such measures as cheating and intimidation.

An invalid labor contract shall have no legal binding force from the very beginning of its conclusion. Where a part of a labor contract is confirmed as invalid and where the validity of the remaining part is not affected, the remaining part shall remain valid.

The invalidity of a labor contract shall confirmed by a labor dispute arbitration committee or a people's court.

Article 19 A labor contract shall be concluded in written form and contain the following

Clauses:

term of a labor contract;
contents of work;
labor protection and working conditions
labor remuneration;
labor discipline;
conditions for the termination of a labor contract; and
responsibility for the violation of a labor contract.

Apart from the required clauses specified in the preceding paragraph, other contents in a labor contract may be agreed upon through consultation by the parties involved.

Article 20 The term of a labor contract shall be divided into fixed term, flexible term or taking the completion of a specific amount of work as a term.

In case a laborer has kept working in a same employing unit for ten years or more and the parties involved agree to extend the term of the labor contract, a labor contract with a flexible term shall be concluded between them if the laborer so requested.

Article 21 A probation period may be agreed upon in a labor contract. The longest probation period shall not exceed six months.

Article 22 The parties involved in a labor contract may reach an agreement in their labor contract on matters concerning keeping he commercial secrets of the employing unit.

Article 23 A labor contract shall terminate upon the expiration of its term or the emergence of the conditions for the termination of the labor contract as agreed upon by the parties involved.

Article 24 A labor contract may be revoked upon agreement reached between the parties involved through consultation.

Article 25 The employing unit may revoke the labor contract with a laborer in any of the following circumstances:

to be proved not up to the requirements for recruitment during the probation period;
to seriously violate labor disciplines or the rules and regulations of the employing units;
to cause great losses to the employing unit due to serious dereliction of duty or engagement in malpractice for selfish ends; and
to be investigated for criminal responsibilities in accordance with the law.

Article 26 In any of the following circumstances, the employing unit may revoke a labor contract but a written notification shall be given to the laborer 30 days in advance:

where a laborer is unable to take up his original work or any new work arranged by the employing unit after the completion of his medical treatment for illness or injury not suffered at work;
where a laborer is unqualified for his work and remains unqualified even after receiving a training or an adjustment to an other work post; and
no agreement on modification of the labor contract can be reached through consultation by the parties involved when the objective conditions taken as the basis for the conclusion of the contract have greatly changed so that the original labor contract can no longer be carried out.

Article 27 During the period of statutory consolidation when the employing unit comes to the brink of bankruptcy or runs deep into difficulties in production and management, and if reduction of its personnel becomes really necessary, the unit may make such reduction after it has explained the situation to the trade union or all of its staff and workers 30 days in advance, solicited opinions from them and reported to the labor administrative department.

Where the employing unit is to recruit personnel six months after the personnel reduction effected according to the stipulations of this Article, the reduced personnel shall have the priority to be re-employed.

Article 28 The employing unit shall make economic compensations in accordance with the relevant provisions of the State if it revokes its labor contracts according to the stipulations in Article 24, Article 26, and Article 27 of this Law.

Article 29 The employing unit shall not revoke its labor contract with a laborer in accordance with the stipulations in Article 26 and Article 27 of this Law in any of the following circumstances:

to be confirmed to have totally or partially lost the ability to work due to occupational diseases or injuries suffered at work;
to be receiving medical treatment for diseases or injuries within the prescribed period of time;
to be a female staff member or worker during pregnant, puerperal, or breast-feeding period; or
other circumstances stipulated by laws, administrative rules and regulations.

Article 30 The trade union of an employing unit shall have the right to air its opinions if it regards as inappropriate the revocation of a labor contract by the unit. If the employing unit violates laws, rules and regulations or labor contracts, the trade union shall have the right to request for reconsideration. Where the laborer applies for arbitration or brings in a lawsuit, the trade union shall render him support and assistance in accordance with the law.

Article 31 A laborer who intends to revoke his labor contract shall give a written notice to the employing unit 30 days in advance.

Article 32 A laborer may notify at any time the employing unit of his decision to revoke the labor contract in any of the following circumstances:

within the probation period;
where the employing unit forces the laborer to work by resorting to violence, intimidation or illegal restriction of personal freedom; or

failure on the part of the employing unit to pay labor remuneration or to provide working conditions as agreed upon in the labor contract.

Article 33 The staff and workers of an enterprise as one party may conclude a collective contract with the enterprise on matters relating to labor remuneration, working hours, rest and vacations, occupational safety and health, and insurance and welfare. The draft collective contract shall be submitted to the congress of the staff and workers or to all the staff and workers for discussion and adoption.

A collective contract shall be concluded by the trade union on behalf of the staff and workers with the enterprise; in an enterprise where the trade union has not yet been set up, such contract shall be also concluded by the representatives elected by the staff and workers with the enterprise.

Article 34 A collective contract shall be submitted to the labor administrative department after its conclusion. The collective contract shall go into effect automatically if no objections are raised by the labor administrative department within 15 days from the date of the receipt of a copy of the contract.

Article 35 Collective contracts concluded in accordance with the law shall have binding force to both the enterprise and all of its staff and workers. The standards on working conditions and labor payments agreed upon in labor contracts concluded between individual laborers and the enterprises shall not be lower than those as stipulated in collective contracts.

Chapter IV Working Hours, Rest and Vacations

Article 36 The State shall practice a working hour system under which laborers shall work for no more than eight hours a day and no more than 44 hours a week on the average.

Article 37 In case of laborers working on the basis of piecework, the employing unit shall rationally fix quotas of work and standards on piecework remuneration in accordance with the working hour system stipulated in Article 36 of this Law.

Article 38 The employing unit shall guarantee that its staff and workers have at least one day off in a week.

Article 39 Where an enterprise can not follow the stipulations in Article 36 and Article 38 of this Law due to its special production nature, it may adopt other rules on working hours and rest with the approval of the labor administrative department.

Article 40 The employing unit shall arrange holidays for laborers in accordance with the law during the following festivals:

the New Year's Day;
the Spring Festival;
the International Labor Day;
the National Day; and
other holidays stipulated by laws, rules and regulations.

Article 41 The employing unit may extend working hours due to the requirements of its production or business after consultation with the trade union and laborers, but the extended working hour for a day shall generally not exceed one hour; if such extension is called for due to special reasons, the extended hours shall not exceed three hours a day under the condition that the health of laborers is guaranteed. However, the total extension in a month shall not exceed thirty six hours.

Article 42 The extension of working hours shall not be subject to restriction of the provisions of Article 41 of this Law under any of the following circumstances:

where emergent dealing is needed in the event of natural disaster, accident or other reason that threatens the life, health and the safety of property of laborers;

where prompt rush repair is needed in the event of breakdown of production equipment, transportation lines or public facilities that affects production and public interests; and

other circumstances as stipulated by laws, administrative rules and regulations.

Article 43 The employing unit shall not extend working hours of laborers in violation of the provisions of this Law.

Article 44 The employing unit shall, according to the following standards, pay laborers remunerations higher than those for normal working hours under any of the following circumstances:

to pay no less than 150 percent of the normal wages if the extension of working hours is arranged;

to pay no less than 200 percent of the normal wages if the extended hours are arranged on days of rest and no deferred rest can be taken; and

to pay no less than 300 percent of the normal wages if the extended hours are arranged on statutory holidays.

Article 45 The State shall practice a system of annual vacation with pay.

Laborers who have kept working for one year and more shall be entitled to annual vacation with pay. The concrete measures shall be formulated by the State Council.

Chapter V Wages

Article 46 The distribution of wages shall follow the principle of distribution according to work and equal pay for equal work.

The level of wages shall be gradually raised on the basis of economic development. The State shall exercise macro-regulations and control over the total payroll.

Article 47 The employing unit shall independently determine its form of wage distribution and wage level for its own unit according to law and based on the characteristics of its production and business and economic results.

Article 48 The State shall implement a system of guaranteed minimum wages. Specific standards on minimum wages shall be determined by the people's governments of provinces, autonomous regions or municipalities directly under the Central Government and reported to the State Council for the record.

Wages paid to laborers by the employing unit shall not be lower than the local standards on minimum wages.

Article 49 The determination and readjustment of the standards on minimum wages shall be made with reference to the following factors in a comprehensive manner:

the lowest living expenses of laborers themselves and the average family members they support;
(2) the average wage level of the society as a whole;
(3) labor productivity;

the situation of employment; and
the different levels of economic development between regions.

Article 50 Wages shall be paid monthly to laborers themselves in form of currency. The wages paid to laborers shall not be deducted or delayed without justification.

Article 51 The employing unit shall pay wages according to law to laborers who observe statutory holidays, take leaves during the periods of marriage or funeral, or participate in social activities in accordance with the law.

Chapter VI Occupational Safety and Health

Article 52 The employing unit must establish and perfect the system for occupational safety and health, strictly implement the rules and standards of the State on occupational safety and health, educate laborers on occupational safety and health, prevent accidents in the process of work, and reduce occupational hazards.

Article 53 Facilities of occupational safety and health must meet the standards stipulated by the State.

Facilities of occupational safety and health installed in new projects and projects to be rebuilt or expanded must be designed, constructed and put into operation and use at the same time as the main projects.

Article 54 The employing unit must provide laborers with occupational safety and health conditions conforming to the provisions of the State and necessary articles of labor protection, and providing regular health examination for laborers engaged in work with occupational hazards.

Article 55 Laborers to be engaged in specialized operations must receive specialized training and acquire qualifications for such special operations.

Article 56 Laborers must strictly abide by rules of safe operation in the process of their work.

Laborers shall have the right to refuse to operate if the management personnel of the employing unit command the operation in violation of rules and regulations or force laborers to run risks in operation; laborers shall have the right to criticize, report or file charges against the acts endangering the safety of their life and health.

Article 57 The State shall establish a system for the statistics, reports and dispositions of accidents of injuries and deaths, and cases of occupational diseases. The labor administrative departments and other relevant departments of the people's governments at or above the county level and the employing unit shall, according to law, compile statistics, report and dispose of accidents of injuries and deaths that occurred in the process of their work and cases of occupational diseases.

Chapter VII Special Protection For Female and Juvenile Workers

Article 58 The State shall provide female workers and juvenile workers with special protection.

°Juvenile workers hereby refer to laborers at the age of 16 but not 18 yet.

Article 59 It is prohibited to arrange female workers to engage in work down the pit of mines, or work with Grade IV physical labor intensity as stipulated by the State, or other work that female workers should avoid.

Article 60 Female workers during their menstrual periods shall not be arranged to engaged in work high above the ground, under low temperature, or in cold water or work with Grade III physical labor intensity as stipulated by the State.

Article 61 Female workers during their pregnancy shall not be arranged to engage in work with Grade III physical labor intensity as stipulated by the State or other work that they should avoid in pregnancy. Female workers pregnant for seven months or more shall not be arranged to extend their working hours or to work night shifts.

Article 62 After childbirth, female workers shall be entitled to no less than ninety days of maternity leaves with pay.

Article 63 Female workers during the period of breast-feeding their babies less than one year old shall not be arranged to engage in work with Grade III physical labor intensity as stipulated by the State or other labor that they should avoid during their breast-feeding period, or to extend their working hours or to work night shifts.

Article 64 No juvenile workers shall be arranged to engage in work down the pit of mines, work that is poisonous or harmful, work with Grade IV physical labor intensity as stipulated by the State, or other work that they should avoid.

Article 65 The employing unit shall provide regular physical examinations to juvenile workers.

Chapter VIII Vocational Training

Article 66 The State shall take various measures through various channels to expand vocational training undertakings so as to develop professional skills of laborers, improve their qualities, and raise their employment capability and work ability.

Article 67 People's governments at various levels shall incorporate the development of vocational training in the plans of social and economic development, encourage and support all enterprises, institutional organizations. Societies and individuals, where conditions permit, to sponsor all kinds of vocational training.

Article 68 The employing unit shall establish a system for vocational training, raise and use funds for vocational training in accordance with the provisions of the State, and provide laborers with vocational training in a planned way and in the light of the actual situation of the unit.

Laborers to be engaged in technical work must receive pre-job training before taking up their posts.

Article 69 The State shall determine occupational classification, set up professional skill standards for the occupations classified, and practice a system of vocational qualification certificates. Examination and verification organizations authorized by the government are in charge of the examination and verification of the professional skills of laborers.

Chapter IX Social Insurance and Welfare

Article 70 The State shall develop social insurance undertakings, establish a social insurance system, and set up social insurance funds so that laborers may receive assistance and compensations under such circumstances as old age, illness, work-related injury, unemployment and child-bearing.

Article 71 The level of social insurance shall be in proportion to the level of social and economic development and the social affordability.

Article 72 The sources of social insurance funds shall be determined according to the categories of insurance, and an overall pooling of insurance funds from the society shall be introduced step by step. The employing unit and laborers must participate in social insurance and pay social insurance premiums in accordance with the law.

Article 73 Laborers shall, in accordance with the law, enjoy social insurance benefits under the following circumstances:

retirement;
illness or injury;
disability caused by work-related injury or occupational disease;
unemployment; and
(5) child-bearing.

The survivors of the insured laborers shall be entitled to subsidies for survivors in accordance with the law.

The conditions and standards for laborers to enjoy social insurance benefits shall be stipulated by laws, rules and regulations.

The social insurance amount that laborers are entitled to, must be timely paid in full.

Article 74 The agencies in charge of social insurance funds shall collect, expend, manage and operate the funds in accordance with the stipulations of laws, and assume the responsibility to maintain and raise the value of these funds.

The supervisory organizations of social insurance funds shall exercise supervision over the revenue and expenditure, management and operation of social insurance funds in accordance with the stipulations of laws.

The establishment and function of the agencies in charge of social insurance funds and the supervisory organizations of social insurance funds shall be stipulated by laws.

No organization or individual shall be allowed to misappropriate social insurance funds.

Article 75 The State shall encourage the employing unit to set up supplementary insurance for laborers according to its practical situations.

The State shall advocate that laborers practice individual insurance in form of saving account.

Article 76 The State shall develop social welfare undertakings, construct public welfare facilities, and provide laborers with conditions for taking rest, recuperation and rehabilitation.

The employing unit shall create conditions so as to improve collective welfare and raise welfare treatment of laborers.

Chapter X Labor Disputes

Article 77 Where a labor dispute between the employing unit and laborers takes place, the parties concerned may apply for mediation or arbitration or take legal proceedings according to law, or may seek for a settlement through consultation. The principle of mediation shall apply to the procedures of arbitration and lawsuit.

Article 78 The settlement of a labor dispute shall follow the principle of legality, fairness and promptness so as to safeguard in accordance with the law the legitimate rights and interests of the parties involved.

Article 79 Where a labor dispute takes place, the parties involved may apply to the labor dispute mediation committee of their unit for mediation; if the mediation fails and one of the parties requests for arbitration, that party may apply to the labor dispute arbitration committee for arbitration. Either party may also directly apply to the labor dispute arbitration committee for arbitration. If one of the parties is not satisfied with the adjudication of arbitration, the party may bring the case to a people's court.

Article 80 A labor dispute mediation committee may be established inside the employing unit. The committee shall be composed of representatives of the staff and workers, representatives of the employing unit, and representatives of the trade union. The chairman of the committee shall be held a representative of the trade union.

The parties involved shall implement agreements reached on labor disputes through mediation.

Article 81 A labor dispute arbitration committee shall be composed of representatives of the labor administrative department, representatives from the trade union at the corresponding level, and representatives of the employing unit. A representative of the labor administrative department shall hold the chairman of the committee.

Article 82 The party that requests for arbitration shall file a written application to a labor dispute arbitration committee within 60 days starting from the date of the occurrence of a labor dispute. The arbitration committee may generally make adjudication within 60 days from the date of receiving the application. The parties involved must implement the adjudication if no objections are raised.

Article 83 Where a party involved in a labor dispute is not satisfied with the adjudication, the party may bring a lawsuit to a people's court within 15 days from the date of receiving the ruling of arbitration. Where one of the parties involved neither brings a lawsuit nor implements the adjudication of arbitration within the statutory time limit, the other party may apply to a people's court for compulsory implementation.

Article 84 Where a dispute arises from the conclusion of a collective contract and no settlement can be reached through consultation by the parties concerned, the labor administrative department of the local people's government may organize the relevant departments to handle the case in coordination.

Where a dispute arises from the implementation of a collective contract and no settlement can be reached through consultation by the parties concerned, the dispute may be submitted to the labor dispute arbitration committee for arbitration. Any party that is not satisfied with the adjudication of arbitration may bring a lawsuit to a people's court within 15 days from the date of receiving the adjudication.

Chapter XI Supervision and Inspection

Article 85 The labor administrative departments of people's governments at or above the county level shall, in accordance with the law, supervise and inspect the implementation of laws, rules and regulations on labor by the employing unit, and have the power to stop any acts that run counter to laws, rules and regulations on labor and order the rectification thereof.

Article 86 The inspectors from the labor administrative departments of people's governments at or above the county level shall, while performing their public duties, have the right to enter the employing units to make investigations about the implementation of laws, rules and regulations on labor examine necessary data and inspect labor sites.

The inspectors from the labor administrative departments of people's governments at or above the county level must show their certifications while performing public duties, impartially enforce laws, and abide by relevant stipulations.

Article 87 Relevant departments of people's governments at or above the county level shall, within the scope of their respective duties and responsibilities, supervise the implementation of laws, rules and regulations on labor by the employing units.

Article 88 Trade unions at various levels shall, in accordance with the law, safeguard the legitimate rights and interests of laborers, and supervise the implementation of laws, rules and regulations on labor by the employing units.

Any organizations or individuals shall have the right to expose and accuse any acts in violation of laws, rules and regulations on labor.

Chapter XII Legal Responsibility

Article 89 Where the rules and regulations on labor formulated by the employing unit run counter to the provisions of laws, rules and regulations, the labor administrative department shall give a warning to the unit, order it to make corrections; where any harms have been caused to laborers, the unit shall be liable for compensations.

Article 90 Where the employing unit extends working hours of laborers in violation of the stipulations of this Law, the labor administrative department shall give it a warning, order it to make corrections, and may impose a fine.

Article 91 Where an employing unit infringes in any of the following ways the legitimate rights and interests of laborers, the labor administrative department shall order it to pay laborers remuneration or to make up for economic losses, and may also order it to pay compensations:

to deduct wages or delay in paying wages to laborers without reason;
to refuse to pay laborers remuneration for the extended working hours;
to pay laborers wages below the local standard on minimum wages; or

to fail to provide laborers with economic compensations in accordance with the provisions of his Law after revocation of labor contracts.

Article 92 Where the occupational safety facilities and health conditions of an employing unit do not comply with the provisions of the State or the unit fails to provide laborers with necessary labor protection articles and labor protection facilities the labor administrative department or other relevant departments shall order it to make corrections, and may impose a fine. If circumstances are serious, the above-said departments shall apply to a people's government at or above the county level for a decision to order the unit to stop production for consolidation. If the unit fails to take measures against potential accident which later leads to the occurrence of a serious accident and the losses of laborers' lives and properties, criminal responsibilities shall be investigated against the persons in charge of the stipulations of Article 187 of the Criminal Law.

Article 93 Where an employing unit forces laborers to operate with risks in violation of the rules and regulations, causing thus major accident of injuries and deaths, and serious consequences, criminal responsibilities of the person in charge shall be investigated according to law.

Article 94 Where an employing unit illegally recruits juveniles under the age of 16, the labor administrative department shall order it to make corrections, and impose a fine. If circumstances are serious, the administrative department for industry and commerce shall revoke its business license.

Article 95 Where an employing unit encroaches upon the legitimate rights and interests of female and juvenile workers in violation of the stipulations of this Law on their protection, the labor administrative department shall order it to make corrections, and impose a fine. If harms to female and juvenile workers have been caused, the unit shall assume the responsibility for compensations.

Article 96 Where an employing unit commits one of the following acts, the person in charge shall be taken by a public security organ into custody for 15 days or less, or fined, given a warning; and criminal responsibilities shall be investigated against the person in charge according to law if the act constitutes a crime;

to force laborers to work by resorting to violence, intimidation or illegal restriction of personal freedom; or
humiliating, giving corporal punishment, bating illegally searching or detaining laborers.

Article 97 The employing unit shall bear the responsibility for compensation if the conclusion of any invalid contracts is attributed to the unit and have caused damages to laborers.

Article 98 The employing unit that revokes labor contracts or purposely delays the conclusion of labor contracts in violation of the conditions specified in this Law shall be ordered by the labor administrative department to make corrections and shall bear the responsibility for compensation if damaged have been caused to laborers.

Article 99 The employing unit that recruits laborers whose labor contracts have not yet been revoked shall, according to law, assume joint responsibility for compensation if economic losses have been caused to the original employing unit of the laborers.

Article 100 The employing unit that fails to pay social insurance premium without reason shall be ordered by the labor administrative department to pay within fixed period of time. If the unit still fails to make the payment beyond the time limit, an additional arrears payment may be demanded.

Article 101 Where an employing unit unjustifiably obstructs the labor administrative department and other relevant departments as well as their functionaries from exercising the powers of supervision and inspection or retaliates informers, the labor administration department or other relevant departments shall impose fines upon the unit. If a crime is constituted, the person in charge shall be investigated for criminal responsibilities according to law.

Article 102 Laborers who revoke labor contracts in violation of the conditions specified in this Law or violate terms on secret-keeping matters agreed upon the labor contracts and thus caused economic losses to the employing unit shall be liable for compensation in accordance with the law.

Article 103 The functionaries of the labor administrative department or other relevant departments who abuse their functions and powers, neglect their duties, and engage in malpractices for selfish ends, shall be investigated for criminal responsibilities according to law if a crime is constituted, or shall be given an administrative sanction if the offences do not yet constitute a crime.

Article 104 The functionaries of the State or the agencies in charge of social insurance funds who misappropriate the social insurance funds, shall be investigated for criminal responsibilities according to law if a crime is constituted.

Article 105 Where other laws or administrative rules and regulations have already specified punishments for the encroachment of the legitimate rights and interests of laborers that also violate the stipulations of this Law, punishments shall be given in accordance with the stipulations of those laws or administrative rules and regulations.

Chapter XIII Supplementary Provisions

Article 106 People's governments of provinces, autonomous regions and municipalities directly under the Central Government shall work out the implementing measures for the labor contract system according to this Law and in light of their local conditions, and report the measures to the State Council for the record.

Article 107 This Law shall become effective as of January 1, 1995

0-595-22622-1

Printed in the United States
16287LVS00002B/175